# Bloodrites of the Post-Structuralists

# Bloodrites of the Post-Structuralists

## WORD, FLESH AND REVOLUTION

ANNE NORTON

**Routledge**
New York • London

Published in 2002 by
Routledge
29 West 35th Street
New York, NY 10001

Published in Great Britain by
Routledge
11 New Fetter Lane
London EC4P 4EE

Routledge is an imprint of the Taylor & Francis Group.

10 9 8 7 6 5 4 3 2 1

Library of Congress Cataloging-in-Publication Data

Norton, Anne.
    Bloodrites of the post-structuralists : word, flesh, and revolution / by Anne Norton.
        p. cm.
    Includes bibliographical references and index.
    ISBN 0-415-93458-3 — ISBN 0-415-93459-1 (pbk.)
        1. Social evolution. 2. Authority. 3. Power (Social sciences) 4. Political development.
    I. Title.

    HM626 .N6785 2002
    303.4—dc21                                                        2002021968

to Roberto Babylon

# Contents

# Acknowledgments

This book took more time than I expected, and over time, came to take fewer pages. As I wrote it became more concentric and eccentric, more formal and less bound within a discipline. I have incurred more debts than I can now recall, yet I have the suspicion that an acknowledgment might be a burden. It is more than usually the case that the errors are mine, and that those whom I thank here are not responsible for my inadequacies and excesses.

I am indebted to Sheldon Wolin, who asked me to give the talk that became the book, at the Huntington Library. I am indebted to Wendy Brown and Judy Butler for their work and conversation, and for inviting me to the Humanities Research Institute of the University of California. The University of Pennsylvania provided research support for this project. Elements and variants of this work were presented at seminars at the University of Chicago, the Massachusetts Institute of Technology, Yale and the Yale Law School, Harvard University, Johns Hopkins University, Amherst College, the New School for Social Research, Princeton University, the University of Texas at Austin, and the University of Pennsylvania. I remember with particular appreciation the help of Robert Ferguson, Owen Fiss, Bruce Ackerman, John McCormick, George Shulman, Austin Sarat, Peter Fitzpatrick, Ann Cvetkovich, Barbara Harlow, Jesse Goldhammer, Lynn Hunt, and Carole Smith-Rosenberg. David Bromwich, Homi Bhabha, Achille Mbembe, William Connolly, and Richard Flathman gave guidance through their work, and in conversation, that I relied on often and have yet to exhaust. I have deep and diverse debts to

Lloyd Rudolph, Susanne Rudolph, Robert Vitalis, Joseph Mink, Ellen Kennedy, Thomas Dumm, Gretchen Ritter, Michael Hanchard, Rogers Smith, Uday Mehta, Victoria Hattam, and Deborah Harrold.

In writing another work, I found that I also had a debt to Routledge, for providing so many of the books I have relied on. As reader and writer, I am grateful to Eric Nelson who continues to advance publishing as an art of provision and provocation.

# Introduction
## A Shape of Life Grown Old

> When philosophy paints its grey in grey
> then has a shape of life grown old.
>
> —Hegel, *Philosophy of Right*

This is a study of a shape of life grown old. The shape belongs to an order whose lineaments, visible in the present, have a presence in the past. The order comprehends within a single structure moments far removed in time. The time recollected here is not linear, not progressive. The order does not advance smoothly or inexorably from one moment to the next. These moments are read like marks on a page, configured in words and sentences, read and read again.

We stand at the horizon of this order, a vantage from which one can see it, not whole perhaps, but as a whole. The order is visible and active in the coupling and opposition, the oscillations and transubstantiations, the rivalries and alliances, between two axes, one constituted between the poles of word and flesh, the other between openness and closure. Flesh encompasses birth, sexuality, and the ties of kinship, violence, mortality, and materiality, body and blood. The word comprehends writing and the text; scripture and constitution; title, dictate, and declaration. Openness is physical, literary, and political, manifest in the bodies of women and in revolution. Closure belongs to systematic reasoning, to orders and institutions, to the bodies of men.

I had at first thought that this would be a succession in which, gradually, irrevocably, the word overcame the flesh, and writing replaced violence. In this progressive, modernist advance the rule of law replaced the

1

rule of men, authority was fixed through words rather than the flow of blood, writing replaced violence, people became ever more disembodied. I saw no such advance. Instead, I found the incarnation casting an iridescence over the nominal triumphs of the word, and flesh that always carries the word inscribed on its inmost parts. I heard the breath in the word. I learned that the form the age took was neither linear nor progressive.

One can find the power of the word over the body enacted in scriptures long antedating law's authority. The dominion of the word is not limited to modernity. Nor does the word enjoy a perfect authority in that moment. The Judeo-Christian scriptures record contracts with Cain, Noah, and Abraham. The word becomes flesh in the rituals of circumcision and the Eucharist. The trials and executions of Charles Stuart and Louis Capet, the emergence of the New Model Army, and the Declaration of Right have been read as moments in the long interrupted advent of modernity. The ascendancy of the word over the flesh, of the rule of law over the rule of men, of lines of scripture over lineages of blood is affirmed here, yet this triumph of scripture is written on the body in regicide and the Terror. Modernity inscribed itself on the body. The discipline of rational legal authority enforced the conformity of the body to written rules and subjected it to the altered rhythms of industrial life. As the body conformed to the machine, it conformed to a machinery of regulation. Drives, appetites, desires, capacities, and defects came to be not only understood but experienced in writing. Word and flesh remain coupled in modernity, in labor and desire, in doing and being.

Each of these axes is subject to the same uncertainties and aporias, the same excesses, that enable all writing to exceed itself. That which defines them marks out a space of difference and uncertainty, of contradiction and aporia, within them. The word, the written, must also contain the work of hand and eye, the speaking mouth and the listening ear. The flesh holds the inscriptions of race and sex, kinship, lineages, bloodright, bloodrites, and blood ties. The scar is a text written on the flesh. Within the word, within the body, openness and closure are coupled. Writing opens as surely as it closes. Closure marks a point of entry and exit, as a closed door remains to mark the way out. Behind the door, beyond the gate, is that which it protects and conceals. The open door determines the point of entry, the open window the direction of the gaze.

Our time is not a rupture with the authority of word and flesh, but an overcoming in which they are simultaneously preserved and surpassed.[1] This is an inquiry into the terms of one moment of our presence. The past constitutes present and future, the present constitutes the past. Each future makes a new past visible. These pasts, once they begin to manifest themselves, are always already present. Weber's modernity is already present in the Scriptural contracts of Cain, Noah, and Abraham. Irigaray's skeptical questioning of Plato and Lacan, Nietzsche and Derrida is already present in the laughter of Sarah. And Althusser has already protested against my reading.

Althusser was right to think that those who opened the world as a text read a fable or, in Freud's words, a "just-so story." These are not tales of our own devising. We read folk tales, fairy tales, that follow the forms "once upon a time" and "there was and there was not." Here I will tell those fables again, on the threshold of the millennium, before we turn away.

There was and there was not a man, imprisoned in the flesh, who refused to remain there. He fled to writing and to the text, but his flesh clung to him like shreds of paper. He could not be free of it. A woman, bearing a note and a knife, opened his body. His blood flowed out, he dropped the pen, and he became a text. Was he dead? Was he transfigured? Was he the author? He was and he was not. This is the story with which I began.

Once there was a closed kingdom in an open sea. This kingdom was under a curse, for everything in it was divided in two. Across the sea was a land that was not land, where people sailed on the streets and farmed the sea, and grew rich on debt. A prince who was not a prince came with an army that was not an army, deposed the foolish king, and opened the kingdom. The prince who was not a prince (but who was a man of his word) married a princess of the blood, and from their marriage came not a royal child but a republican text.

There are other stories, more often told than these, whose effects reveal the authority of this fabulous form.

Once there was a man who had a son he loved. God called to the man and said, "Take your son, whom you love, take him up on the mountain and make him a burnt offering to me, for I am the Lord your God." The man took his son and went on the mountain and built a funeral pyre. There are more endings to this story than are spoken aloud. Usually, it is said that the man came down again with his son alive, and that the god spared the son. Some, hearing this, wonder whether the god spared the son, or the man defied his god, or the man's faith died on the funeral pyre. Some think that he killed his son and the tale has not the heart to tell us. This last is, I think, the story as Fanon tells it.

All the episodes within this book might be told in this way. In each of them there is a structure, that of necessary changeability, that holds the variants in a relation of kinship to each other. Behind and before each story is another whose silent text can be read in the spaces between the words. Within each story are the lines that enable it to be told again differently. They echo in the absence of that telling. Within each story is a question, a thought posed in the interval between the present form and the absent variants. There is authority in these stories, in these words and the forms they follow, but no author. Each telling differs as it carries the form forward. In each telling one hears the critique of the nymph Echo.

My work here is to give flesh to the violence of the letter, to make the word's closure of the body palpable, to show that the seemingly precious and all too literary constructs of the poststructuralists have a presence in the flesh, and that these are matters not of the word but of the world. The violence of the letter takes its political form in the cahiers and in lettres de cachet. The pain of Damiens inscribes itself in the writing of Foucault, the once-Algerian writes of being *sous rature*. The death of the author and the dissemination of authority find their political forms in regicide and the Terror, in the peasants who soaked their bread in the blood of Louis Capet, and the burned cafés of Algiers.

These are the bloodrites of the poststructuralists. The guillotine is the instrument of the death of the author. The deaths of kings and colonists underwrite the constitutions of republics. The sex that is not one is formed in the vortex of desire that begets the Orient. These are not mere echoes and translations of greater acts long over; the sublime become ridiculous, the decadent descendants of a once dangerous house. The work of these revolutions is incomplete. Changes to the literary mind will change the body politic in time.

There is another history—a future past—written in the texts before us. In this already written history, words become flesh and flesh becomes words with a rapidity that makes them iridescent. The attributes of closure and openness have become detached from the masculine and feminine bodies on which they were once so firmly fixed. The enthralling stabilities of gender have come undone, unwinding, like Draupadi's sari, into a fabulous instability.

Look again at Sarah. Here the annunciation comes to a man; ear and mind replace the womb, and the child is first conceived in Abraham. Here the wound of circumcision, the lack at the site of sexuality, becomes a sign of authority and title to power. Look again in Sade. There is more there than meets the eye. Sade announces a somatic economy in which one orifice may be readily exchanged for another and men's bodies are as open as women's. Look again at Draupadi. The attempt to strip her bare becomes the unwinding of a shroud, the unrolling of a scroll. Much has been written on those unrolled sheets, and still there is more to write.

In the myths of Demeter and Sarah, in Sade, Irigaray, and Derrida, one can see another past that has not yet become our past. This is the past of an order different from that which has been our own. This past belongs not to what we have been but to what we will become, to what we are not yet. Nothing that I can say about this should surprise you. In this past, which still lies in our future, the absence of closure—the open text, the empty womb—is not seen simply as lack but as the site of lack and fecundity. The signs of sexuality that once fixed meaning in bodies now serve as currency in a somatic economy of circulation and exchange.

The very familiarity of these observations suggests to me that this order has already come to be our own.

# Section 1

# 1
## Power in the Blood

anguage is the field of our being. Our thoughts are cast into language before their conception; we are born into language before we are born to the world. Our bodies are not simply flesh. They are incarnations, for in them the word precedes the flesh. They bear meaning before they are borne in the womb. Arm, hand, head, and heart existed for us before we had arms and hands and heads and hearts to occupy them. Our bodies are already constituted before we enter them. Whatever shape the body takes, the meaning of that shape is there before it.

The field marked out by the poles of word and flesh unites modernity and tradition in a single order as it opposes each to the other. The canonical identification of tradition with the flesh, modernity with the word (so easily undone), has an uncanny persistence, for each is maintained by serving as its own changeling. Transubstantiation drives the opposition forward. The embodiment of power in traditional authority—power in the blood—finds a form in words as well. Within the moment of the word's ascendancy, the inscription of power on the flesh continues. In each of these epochs—in modernity, in tradition—a constitutional schematic of word and flesh is read in, and inscribed on, sexed bodies. Meanings become incarnate in the inscription of sexed political hierarchies on the silent, passionate, and resistant flesh. The flesh becomes the name.

Names, we know, are not mere ornaments, subject to the forms they mark. The name of woman gives the diverse bodies and experiences of women a common name, and in that name a common form. The names of race and nation carry histories and hierarchies within them. The name of the father carries authority, subjection, and a blessing. In each instance, the name elaborates itself, acquiring an internal richness, writing its exegeses on the bodies named. The name, the word, carries the variety and the insistent demands of the flesh within it. The word, loosed from the flesh, carrying the breath of the flesh within it, circulates. Man and woman, masculine and feminine, hand and eye, stomach and sex come to rest not only on the bodies of men and women but on the political bodies of states, colonies, and empires.

The commentaries that follow are written on this site: on the named and naming body as an exegetical text, and on the strategies the topography of that site demands.

Traditional authority was described by Weber as "patriarchal." It is and it is not. Traditional authority is not a system based simply upon the authority of the paterfamilias. Weber's reading attends to the peaceful transmission of property, but it neglects the way in which property and status were acquired, maintained, extended, and lost. Traditional authority is based not on kinship alone but on bloodlines, blood ties. In such systems, authority is established and transmitted in two ways: through violence and through sexuality.

When Oliver Cromwell called Charles Stuart the "Man of Blood," he alluded not merely to his lineage nor to his acts of violence, but to the substance of his authority.[1] Under traditional forms of legitimate domination, war establishes the limits, the boundaries, of the nation. The making of war was the calling of the monarch and the nobility. The accouterments of war served as signifiers of rank. Kings were portrayed in armor, carrying weapons as signs of sovereignty. War determined status and the ownership of land. Princes and aristocrats trained for war in hunting, they contended with one another in duels. These activities were forbidden to the common people for authority flowed through the blood of man and beast.

Blood flows, in this understanding, not only on the battlefield but between men and women in sex, between the mother and the child in her womb and at her breast, between one generation and the next. The shedding of blood in intercourse, particularly the blooding that was thought to mark the end of virginity, united families and marked the husband's authority over his wife. The sheet from the marriage bed, marked with the woman's blood, was the text of her subjection. Her husband held it as his title to her. Inheritance followed the blood ties of kinship and sexuality. The child's title was held in the child's blood. The passage of blood from one generation to the next was accomplished in myriad mechanisms of transubstantiation and transfusion. The child in the mother's womb was formed of the father's blood in semen, fed on the blood of the mother. After birth, the child was nourished on the mother's blood, transmuted into milk.[2]

The display of sexuality in dress and manners—indeed, in the act itself—was formalized in the social practices of the aristocracy. The consummation of royal marriages and the births of princes were spectacles, visible at least to the highest of the aristocracy. The nobility, in accordance with their descending rank, were permitted (and encouraged in) less conspicuous sexual displays. With violence, sexuality was the alphabet of authority at court.

A satiric etching from the early years of the French Revolution makes this point quite bluntly. Marie Antoinette is shown in the classic position of Baubo. Lafayette, whose loyalty to the Revolution is impugned by the etching, kneels to her, with his hand on her sex. The caption reads "Ma Constitution."[3] Lafayette is presented as rejecting the authority of writing for the authority of the flesh, vested here in the queen's sex.

The classic dichotomy of men as warriors, women as wombs, which appears first as an opposition, conceals a diverted inversion. Men, who endeavored to retain their blood in warfare, acquired authority in spilling the blood of others. Women, whose bodies regularly spilled their blood, acquired authority when they retained it. Virgins, celestial and terrestrial, retain their integrity with their blood. Mothers, retaining in their bodies the blood that is normally spilled monthly, acquire authority in the making and nourishment of the child.

This is not, however, the simple inversion that it first appears. Men spilled not their own blood (as women commonly did) but the blood of others. Women kept not only their own blood (as men did) but the blood of another: father and child. The pregnant woman holds the embryo's blood within her own, and it is from the father's blood in semen that the embryo grows, fed on her own. The separation of the shedding of blood from its retention marked the separation of women and men. The inversion of this order, whereby men spilled and women kept blood, constructed male power as violence, feminine power as sexuality.

In this sanguinary economy, women nourish, men wound. Women give life, men take it away. Women preserve the order, passing power from one generation to the next. Men alter that order, interrupting the steady flow of blood in the vein, and channel power elsewhere. Yet this ordered inversion of the qualities that separate men from women is diverted. The system is secured not when the woman keeps her own blood, but when she keeps the blood of another, not when the man spills his blood, but when he spills the blood of another. It is this diversion of the inverted function onto another that makes the household an economy of blood, and provides the signs that ensure its unity.

It is also this diversion that makes feminine adultery threatening and masculine adultery insignificant. The woman, who is to retain the seed of the father and pass on his blood with her own, might spill that blood in abortion, or replace it with the blood of another in adultery. In these acts, the bloodlines follow her will. The child of another man's blood and the mother's choice will have authority in the flesh, but only while he bears the name of the man who is not his father and the woman keeps her secret. It is in its capacity for secrecy that the woman's body retains the potential for transgressive authority. Here, with the recognition of the secret authority of the body, aristocracy is identified as feminine. Here, in time, the partisans of liberalism will make their claim to the name of the father, as they open the secret places and secure authority through the word.

The security not only of the economy of blood but of male authority within it is established by a diversion. The power that passes with the flow of blood in war, in hunting and dueling, and in sex moves immediately to the man who sheds it. The power that a woman may possess by governing the flow of blood is, however, displaced and deferred. The mother gains an immediate power over the child in her womb and at her breast. It is subject to her authority, it is put immediately in her power, yet the child who bears the name of the father is within paternal authority before his birth.

The danger—and the appeal—of the mother's power in the flesh is vividly evident in Machiavelli's account of Caterina Sforza. Sforza had been captured by those besieging her city but was permitted to visit Forli, leaving her children as hostages, in order to persuade the intractable citizens to surrender. Once within the gates, Sforza appeared on the battlements, shouting her defiance. She was reminded that her children were held hostage. Raising her skirts, she showed her sex and proclaimed, "With this I can make many more."[4] In this gesture, Caterina Sforza asserted the power of her body. "Every woman that bears children, becomes both a *mother* and a *lord*," Hobbes wrote, for "every man is supposed to promise obedience, to him in whose power it is to save or destroy him."[5] Modernity would make servants of mothers, but Caterina Sforza saw her maternity as a source of power and an avenue to rule. Sforza's defiant display of the site and instrument of her authority makes the sight of feminine sexuality a weapon. Her laughter on the barricades is the laughter of the Medusa.

Her power is the power to make and unmake.[6] Hobbes saw it. The conventional subjection of women required childbearing women to abandon their power in the flesh for a contractual authority. Hobbes transforms the authority of the women over the child from blood right to contract. This reading of the mother's authority gave it temporal limits and transformed the mother's right to kill or abandon her child into a gate whereby male authority might enter. Hobbes ascribed the mother's decision to nurture the child to her own interests and inclinations. From it, she would derive an unquestionable dominion. This was not, however, the only reading that this economy of word and flesh could bear. The woman was also read as possessing authority only while her blood flows to the child. She has it only in the flesh. Motherhood, in that time as in this, enthralls the mother as well as the child. Here too power follows blood. The mother is bound to the child who draws blood from her, not once but many times. The man's authority, by contrast, is understood as writing; it leaves a mark. The blood he sheds continues to mark his assumption of authority after it has ceased to flow. He has authority in his absence. She is present and subject in her presence.

The authority of the man who becomes a father by choosing to nurture an abandoned child is presented by Hobbes as identical to that of the woman who might have raised the child. Each, enjoying the power of life and death, enters into a contractual relation with the child, who is obliged by the preservation of his life to defer to this power over him.

The contractarian recognition of maternal power in the blood occurs only with the replacement of bodily with contractual dominion. The possibility of a prior feminine authority is broached, from Hobbes to Bachofen, only when it has already been superseded. Feminine sexuality, the site of the womb, came to be read not as the site of power but as the source of powerlessness and occupation. The woman's sex was her occupation. It was what she did for a living, and it marked what was done to her. She was occupied—in the Freudian and military senses—by the phallus. This occupation was politically significant because it asserted the superiority of violence to sexuality and of masculine to feminine in the determination of authority. Yet if the womb was the location of woman's powerlessness in her occupation by the phallus, it was also the place out of which her power might come: a place of *potentia*.

It is on the site of the womb that the authority of the phallus is established. It is on the site of the womb that the authority of the phallus is revealed as the authority of writing. The woman held her authority over blood in the flesh. The man held his authority through writing. Each authoritative act proper to men left a trace: the mark of blood, or a scar, in war; the mark of the seed in the woman's body. The child who might (or might not) be his in the flesh was marked as his by name. The right he held in the flesh, by blood, was secured by writing. This dependence upon, and consequently capacity for, writing differentiates the claims of men and women under traditional authority. It provides insight into one of the axes of traditional and rational legal authority, and suggests why—in the order of word and flesh—the authority ascribed to women is put under erasure with the advent of the letter.

# 2
## Closed Body, Open Mind

Modern political authority is based (so it tells us) on writing, on logos: on the word and the law. Modernity has given itself scriptural origins. Modern authority sees in itself the triumph of the word, and gives itself a scriptural genealogy. "In the beginning was the word." Contract and the sign carry divine authority in scripture. God signs the body of Cain. The covenant of God with Noah is marked by a sign in the sky, the covenant with Abraham by another sign on the flesh. The deity declares, "I will write my law on your inmost parts"; the prophet swallows the honeyed text. Among Christians, "the word became flesh and dwelt among us." That flesh becomes a sign. The sign consumed transforms human bodies into a scriptural community. Among Protestants, the community is formed not by the body of Christ consumed but by the word of God. The divine would no longer enter the flesh through the flesh but through the reading eye, the listening ear, the believing mind. Scripture was the dictate of a silent but nevertheless legible divinity. Submission to the rule of laws rather than the rule of men marked the progress of the word in the world.

That which has its advent in the Protestant ethic and the spirit of capitalism has its epiphany in the literary quotidian of modern life. The primacy of the word over the flesh manifests itself in the authority of documents and the ubiquity of contracts. Contracts bind the flesh in slavery, in marriage. Capitalism is profoundly literary: each piece of money is a small text on trust affirming the state's authority. Yet capitalism does not leave the flesh behind. The scriptural text "and the Word was made flesh, and dwelt among us" echoes in Weber's observation that the machine is the command made material. The descent of clerks from clerics, of capitalism from Protestantism, of contracts and bureaucracy from scripture and the primacy of writing can be read with equal ease in texts and institutions. Foucault's recognition of the impulse to confession, the imperative to cast oneself into language, Derrida's insistence on the primacy of the written, and Kojeve's declaration that we are all becoming ever more Japanese belong in this chronicle of the ascendancy of writing.

We are written people, with literary selves.

Women were excluded at the outset from the contracts and constitutions that were the medium of rational legal authority. Writing was denied them, as writings by them were denied. Yet women were constructed as the object and the occasion for the writings of the modern age. For rational legal authority, as for traditional authority, woman is the emptiness at the center. Yet woman is present at the point of origin. The modern origin myths of the social contract and the primal horde are written on her body.

Modernity is the epoch of liberalism, of the ascendancy of contract. It is liberalism that claims to be the epoch of "liberty, equality, and fraternity." The third term would seem sufficient to refute any pretensions to the first two. Liberalism, however, has continued to mark feminine subjection as a residue of traditional authority, even as it secured and extended it.

The subjection of women is, however, neither archaic nor foreign to liberalism. The participation of women in the liberal revolutions of the eighteenth and nineteenth centuries was rewarded with more limited influence, more thorough formal and informal regulation. The great liberal revolutions marked the triumph of liberty by securing a more exclusive fraternity. Women who had stormed the Tuileries with the sans-culottes found themselves denied admission to Jacobin clubs.[1]

Tocqueville observed, and commended, the stricter confinement of women in America, their more thorough exclusion from public discourse and political influence. Americans, Tocqueville wrote, have never "supposed that democratic principles should undermine the husband's authority . . . they never deny him the right to direct his spouse."[2] "Thus, then, while they have allowed the social inferiority of woman to continue, they have done everything to raise her morally and intellectually to the level of man. In this I think they have wonderfully understood the true conception of democratic progress."[3] Tocqueville's analysis places the conventional subjection of women at the center of the liberal project. Sexual hierarchies are presented in Tocqueville not as a feudal aberration but as a liberal principle.

The classic texts of liberalism present conceptions of contract, individuality, and liberty that inscribe subjection on the woman's body. Liberalism marked bodily integrity as the sign and security of liberty. Liberals undertook to protect men's bodies, even from themselves. Hobbes made contract the guarantor of bodily integrity and the sovereign the security of that state, and proscribed even attacks upon oneself. Man might live with his body closed to the intrusions of others, and in that safety he would find his freedom. Hobbes, and Locke after him, made the body fence and shelter for the mind. Men free from fear could look beyond survival. Men with their bodies inviolable, protected from assaults by other men, could think for themselves. The closed body sheltered the open mind.

In Locke, the incorporative body served as the means and model for understanding the acquisition of property. Taking in goods empowered the individual and extended his dominion with his will into the world, into time. The closed body sheltered the extended will.

The open body was the body subjected. The body that was open to the assaults of others held a mind occupied by fear, beliefs subject to coercion. Any body that depended on another for subsistence might be made the other's subject. An intrusion that could touch the stomach would touch the heart. Opening the body closed the mind.

The bodies borne by women were open bodies. Theirs were bodies that opened in sex, in the conception and the birth and the feeding of children. Theirs were bodies others occupied. Theirs were bodies the law held open to husbands. The bodies of men might be opened by violence, marked and made subject, but women's bodies were seen as open from their birth. They could be properly closed only when they were coupled with men's, or confined in the fictive body of the household.[4]

Liberalism vested rights and authority in the body and provided protection to it. One held rights in, and acquired property through, the body. British and American common law recognized the importance of the body's presence in its provision for habeas corpus and in securing the right to confront one's accusers in the flesh. A plethora of laws aimed at securing the ends named in the American Constitution "to provide for the common defense and promote the general welfare."

Not only individual but collective power and title originated in the body. Authority and legitimacy originated in the people assembled.

The state itself must defer to the authority called up in the present bodies of the assembled people. The privileging of speech that Derrida observed in the high regard of liberal regimes for epics and anthems is the sign that an all too literary liberalism locates itself in the body, achieving the synthesis of representation and authority "in the self presence of its speech."[5]

Liberalism acted through the law to acknowledge and to secure the integrity of the body as security for the integrity of the mind sheltered within it. It endeavored to close off the bodies of men from one another and to maintain these bodies in a state thought to be inviolable and impenetrable. The bodies of women, which were thought to be naturally open, were closed off civilly, in marriage and the household. Women's bodies, naturally open, achieved the closure that ensured their integrity only when they were comprehended within the name and authority of their husbands.

The state of the liberal individual, endowed with rights, bearing a mind thought to be open in a body closed to the intrusions of others, was "biologically," "naturally" foreclosed to women. The liberal individual was singular. Pregnancy would make some women's bodies momentarily plural. The necessity of closing the bodies of women made their plurality constant, encompassing women in the names and will of their fathers and husbands. The liberal individual was autonomous. Women could not be permitted this autonomy lest they act against the interests of those they held in their bodies or those who held them in the household.

There are two other sets of bodies made subject by their openness. Liberalism's conception of the political consequences of corporeality required not only the exclusion of women from the public sphere but also the stricter regulation of male sexual conduct in the (nominally) private sphere. Men who opened their bodies to other men lost the inviolable, impenetrable interiority of the body that secured rights. The subordination of male homosexuals differs from that of women, however, for it was seen as determined not by providence but by choice. Female subjection was natural. Male subjection was "unnatural" and in defiance of providence.

The imperial ventures of liberalism from the seventeenth through the twentieth centuries reinforced the connection between domination and the opening of the body. Colonies were established by the desire for and the penetration of the other, the "opening up" of the body politic. The discourse of colonialism personified both empire and the colony (and imperialists and colonists) in terms of open and closed, masculine and feminine. The colonized were read as open, identified either as feminine or as open, penetrable, male bodies.

The bodies of women, male homosexuals, and the colonized, alike in the openness ascribed them, different in the understanding of its origin and duration, were alike in another respect as well. The open body was the body of indiscriminate, unbounded desire. Male homosexuals were constructed as promiscuous, imperial possessions as realms of unrestrained sexuality. Women, Rousseau warned, have "insatiable desires." Were they not restrained by shame and the law, "men would be tyrannized by women." For given the ease with which women arouse men's senses "and reawaken in the depths of their hearts the remains of ardors which are almost extinguished, men would be their victims and would see themselves dragged to death without ever being able to defend themselves."[6]

The open body is the body of desire—the desired and desiring body. All bodies are subject to desire: to hunger, to lust, to longing, to all forms of wanting. The feminine body, already marked as open, becomes the mark of irresolute desire. The ascription of insatiability to women exceeds and supplements liberalism. Freud asks, "What do women want?" having already determined that women are always wanting something. Desire marks the presence of an aporia. This lack, this desire, is turned in modernity to the promise of disembodiment.

The nominal integrity of the male body is no more (though no less) than that. Men's bodies are also open and plural. They desire, and they are the objects of desire. Desiring, they experience incompletion, lack, irresolution. They share—prior to their birth—in the collective corporeality of gestation. They eat: they are neither impenetrable nor inviolable.

Classical republicans recognized that the economic structures of an emergent capitalism put the security of individual provision—and therefore individual liberty—at hazard. Their concern for securing universal access to the means of provision was entirely consonant with the liberal arguments that had made the closed body security for the open mind. These too-corporeal republicans failed, however, to recognize what contract had accomplished. The merely nominal integrity of the male body served as currency for the open mind.

With the advent of contract, men had entered upon civil society, and in doing so had imposed upon themselves the authority of representation. "Things inanimate," Hobbes argued, "cannot be authors, nor therefore give authority to their actors: yet the actors may have authority to procure their maintenance, given them by those that are owners, or governors of those things. And therefore, such things cannot be personated, before there be some state of civil government."[7] The establishment of civil government, however, makes representation authoritative and impersonation legitimate. The advent of civil society is the advent of representation. The interests and the will of the people are represented by contract and sovereignty. Representation replaces the body. Through it, the presence of authority can be secured in the absence of the assembled people. Representation becomes the medium of politics and commerce: money becomes currency for goods and value, title currency for rights and property, contract currency for will.

Individuality, in an embodied liberalism, has the status of an attribute. It presents itself as merely a trait or quality, a representation of one aspect of a person, that held in common with all other men. Where representation has authority, liberalism is disembodied. Individuality is no longer an attribute of embodied men but a status or condition, detached from the bodies that were once its source.

The liberal individual, bearing rights, holding an open mind secure in a closed body, became an abstraction. Individuality, once an attribute of certain bodies, became an abstraction assignable to any body, and to no body. Corporations, lacking the embodiment—much less the bodily integrity—that individuality once designated, acquired that status in law. Men, who had once held rights in their bodies, who had made their bodies the title and the means to citizenship, now supplemented those nominally natural rights with the creation of literary selves. The idea of individuality overcomes the represented bodies of men, replacing that which it purported to represent.

Disembodiment removed liberalism one step further from the inscription of rank at birth that had marked feudalism. Disembodiment moved liberalism one step closer to the rule of reason. Yet these bodies, constituted in writing before they were constituted in the flesh, continued to be read as closed or open, masculine or feminine. These attributes, once thought to be corporeal, revealed themselves as qualities not of the bodies but of the texts written on and read into them. The authority of writing over the body and the ascendancy of contract over the flesh in the determination of status did little to elevate the status of women.

Locke's *Two Treatises on Government* present themselves as a confrontation with Patriarchal authority. Locke challenges Filmer's conflation of monarchy and a primordial patriarchy. Recurring, as Filmer had done, to scripture, he observed that Filmer had warped the words of the divine commandment.

> For had our A. set down this Command without Garbling, as God gave it, and joyned *Mother* to Father, every Reader would have seen that it made directly against him, and that it was so far from Establishing the *Monarchical Power of the Father,* that it set up the *Mother* equal with him.[8]

Locke did not proceed, as Filmer had done, from the interpretation of scripture to the ascription of right. He remarks of the subjection of women to their husbands that though it might be imposed by God,

> there is here no more Law to oblige a Woman to such a Subjection, if the Circumstances either of her Condition or Contract should exempt her from it, then there is, that she should bring forth her Children in Sorrow and Pain, if there could be found a Remedy for it.[9]

Woman's subjection is accomplished, in Locke's account, by contract and her condition.[10] A condition once ascribed to providence is now ascribed to the woman's own volition. Contract, which serves to liberate men in Locke's account, is made the apology for women's subjection.

Rousseau's account of twice-born man, who in the second birth is made a citizen, rests on the construction of woman.[11] In Rousseau's account sexual contract accompanies (if it does not precede) social contract. In a few short paragraphs in the "Discourse on Political Economy" Rousseau strips women of their authority and hands it first to fathers, then to the state. The father should rule in the family, Rousseau argues, because he provides for it (an arrogation of a feminine capacity), because he is not subject to "the incapacities peculiar to the wife," and finally because "it is important to him that the children he is forced to recognize do not belong to anyone other than himself. The wife, who has no such thing to fear, does not have the same right over her husband."[12] Here the father's authority over the children is acknowledged by Rousseau to be the product of convention and law. He is forced to recognize, and to support, those children his wife bears to carry his name. His authority is the authority of names, contract, and the law.[13] As such, it is inferior to the authority of the state. The state, Rousseau writes, will acquire the fathers' rights by fulfilling their duties. In doing so, it acquires the comprehensive capacity and authority of the mother. The state becomes, "the tender mother who nourishes them."[14]

The dependence of the social contract on the subjection of women pervades Rousseau's writings on politics and education. The transformation of Emile from man to citizen is dependent upon his education in domestic matters. Emile must be taught to desire Sophie. The practices that bind him to her will bind him to his nation: "it is the good husband and the good father who makes the good citizen." It is through women that men are subjected. Emile subjects himself in his desire. Rousseau tells us that should he learn he can satisfy himself, all is lost, for he will be dependent on no other.[15] It is through desire for women that men are rendered tractable, governable.

There are, however, two moments in which men might be subjected to women. The first, which Hobbes bluntly acknowledged, is the condition into which they are born, the moment of physical dependence on the body of the woman. Men, Rousseau declares, are born free. This is a telling lie. Men are born into the authority of women. The dependent child is nursed and, as Rousseau insists, receives its first and most important education at the hands of women. Why does this dependence not subject it? If the child—the male child—is born free, it is because he is born to one who is already his servant. The woman's care for her male child is thus not an act of authority but the rendering of service due at birth. If men are born free, it is because women are subjected, for otherwise theirs would be the authority. If men are born free, they are born always and already named as agents, constituted in language, for they remain subject in the flesh.

The second of the mythic contracts that founds the modern age is also made a rebellion against patriarchal authority. Darwin speculated that human society consisted, in the first instance, of "a violent and jealous father who keeps all the females for himself and drives away his sons as they grow up."[16] One day, Freud continues, "the brothers who had been driven out came together, killed and devoured their father and so made an end of the patriarchal horde."[17] This "memorable and criminal deed," as Freud calls it, was the beginning not only of contract but of "social organization, of moral restrictions, and of religion."[18] It was done, Freud tells us in his "just-so story," for the possession of women.

Freud wrote in explicit opposition to J. J. Atkinson's theory of contract in *Primal Law*. Atkinson had suggested that the transition to contract was effected "through the intervention of maternal love." The mother's intercession enabled the sons to remain with the horde and "in return for this toleration the sons acknowledged their father's sexual privilege." Like Freud's extension of the Darwinian myth, Atkinson places the figure of the woman at the center, here as the active initiator of, as well as the occasion for, the contract. Freud writes of Atkinson's account, "In its essential feature it is in agreement with my own; but its divergence results in its failing to effect a correlation with many other issues."[19] First among these is the position of woman. The killing of the father, in both accounts, inaugurates the rule of the ideal, and the escape of the dominion of the body. It marks the advent of contract. Atkinson's account, however, imputes to women an actively authoritative role not consonant with their diminished and subordinate place in the structures of rational legal authority. When Freud recounts the myth of the killing of the father in *Group Psychology and the Analysis of the Ego* he again makes reference to an account that suggests the possible centrality of maternal authority, this time from Ferenczi. As with Atkinson, he dismisses the account. Freud's continued reiterations of this possibility, followed by denial, suggest the necessity of putting woman under erasure.[20]

In the Freudian myth of contract, women, the initial possessors of the phallus, are rendered mere signs for authority. The possession of women is made the mark of power, the sign of the rule of men. Woman is made the emptiness at the center. She figures as an object of desire, as lack.

In the order of the word, of logos, law and language, woman figures as the occasion for contract, as the pretext to the text. She figures as mouth to speech, as speech to writing, as the mouth to the hand. She is the counterpart to male writing. As the pretext to the text, as speech to writing, and as the mouth to the hand, she is that which writing supplements, and as supplement, replaces.[21]

The image of the woman, the image of the open mouth, counterposes the absence of closure to definition. This is the site of the origin of the symbolic order, the birth of language, and consciousness. It is this reading of what Courbet called "l'origine du monde" that Nietzsche relies on when he writes, "Perhaps Truth is a woman who has reasons for not letting us see her reasons. Perhaps her name is—to speak Greek—Baubo."[22]

In each case, whether of the rule of blood or the rule of the word, the feminine figures not merely as the counterpart of male authority but as that which male authority must overcome. She is construed as a necessary prerequisite, valuable only insofar as one can distance oneself from it. In traditional systems, feminine authority is subjected through the assertion of violence over sexuality (an assertion that continues to be made, figuratively and literally, in the modern world). In the rational world of the written law, women likewise stand for that which must be overcome.

The woman's sex figures in tradition and modernity as a sign of inferiority, of the lack of power, and as the occasion for subjection. Yet the construction of these systems reveals the inscription of feminine sexuality not as a sign but as a cipher. In the language of politics woman is made the sign of lack, the zero, the emptiness at the center, around which both scriptural and political authority are built. Like the zero, woman is to be independently valueless, enhancing tenfold the value of any sign with which it is coupled. Woman is made the sign of dependent and contingent value, meaningless in itself. If woman is to be read, it must be as a cipher, of indeterminate meaning, perpetually open to change and interpretation, the appropriate object of deconstruction.

The sign "woman" is thus too much and not enough. "Woman" is not adequate to the experiences, the attributes, the differences of women. Yet "woman" is also too full, replete with contradictory attributes, always available to subordinate those it names. The recognition of the indeterminacy of "woman," of the feminine cipher, might seem to leave women once again lacking: lacking a name, lacking an identity. Accepting this indeterminacy might seem a retreat from a generation of efforts to recover a past, and with that past open a future. That has not been the case. Feminist theory's unsettling of sex and sexuality, and the tactics of many political women and men, have made the emptiness at the center of "woman" fertile and productive. The privileging of closure is challenged by poststructuralists, by gay rights activists, and by feminists who refuse both definitive histories and compulsory heterosexuality. The ascription of integrity to the masculine body has been challenged by environmentalists, animal rights activists, queer theory, and gay politics and practice. These movements, political and academic, contest, in different sites, the economy of openness and closure in which contemporary political bodies are constituted.

# 3
# The Word Made Flesh: Barbarities

I n the economy of closure and openness, word and flesh, the colonized belong to the body, open to intrusions, interventions, invasion. Imprisoned within the body, they were outside the logos, foreign to both the law and the word. They were, for the soi-disant descendants of the Greek polis who came to be their rulers, barbarians, those whose speech cannot be understood.

Hegel wrote in the introduction to the *Philosophy of History,* "At this point we leave Africa, not to mention it again. For it is no historical part of the World. . . . What we properly understand by Africa, is the Unhistorical, Undeveloped Spirit, still involved in the conditions of mere nature."[1]

For Hannah Arendt, at the close of the era of imperial dominion, Africa remained outside the logos, "still involved in the conditions of mere nature." Africa was an empty place, "the silent wilderness of an overpopulated continent where the presence of human beings only underlined utter solitude."[2] In that place beyond the logos, there was no history. Europeans confronted "tribes of which they have no historical record and which do not know any history of their own."[3] There was no politics. Shaka had "established neither a people nor a nation": "Since discipline and military organization by themselves cannot establish a political body, the destruction remained an unrecorded episode in an unreal, incomprehensible process which cannot be accepted by man and therefore is not remembered by human history."[4] Lacking history, politics, language, Arendt could only say of Africans: "they had not created a human world."[5] In this she agreed with Marx's assessment: "they cannot represent themselves, they must be represented."

Marx's verdict, which Said made the epigraph of *Orientalism,* captures the political subjection entailed in the nominal alienation of the colonized from the word. Foreign to the word, they lacked authority. They could not—or would not be permitted to—represent themselves in politics. Those who would represent them would be not merely foreign but of a different kind. Their representatives would be those who could represent not only themselves but others. The subjection of the colonized conferred a more than double authority on their rulers. Those who would represent the colonized claimed a capacity for knowledge and action comprehensive enough to include not only themselves but those they claimed to represent. Their claim mirrored the claim of empire. This comprehensive authority was not confined to state politics. This was an order of subjection whose boundaries extended far beyond the institutions of the state.

The colonized were subjected in writing, subjects of it, subject to it. The voluminous files of secretariats and foreign offices were not only the record but the means of government. "The whole government of India is carried out in writing," Mill testified.[6] We are all in language, as Gadamer observed, but not all in the same way. In his elegant, subversive appropriation of the ancient mythology of speaking and writing, Homi Bhabha captures the particular place of the colonized in liberalism's linguistic imaginary: "If the spirit of the Western nation has been symbolized in epic and anthem, voiced by 'a unanimous people assembled in the self-presence of its speech,' then the sign of colonial government is cast in a lower key, caught in the irredeemable act of writing."[7] The colonized were written—written on, written of, written for, written into flesh—but never writing, never speaking, denied utterance, denied the capacity for dictat and declaration.

Edward Said's *Orientalism* has become the canonical examination of the writing of the subject colonized. In Orientalism, as Said recognized, the confluence of political and literary authority is particularly visible. Orientalism, Said wrote, is an academic discipline, a "style of thought" that serves "as the starting point for elaborate theories, epics, novels, social descriptions, and political accounts," and "a corporate institution for dealing with the Orient—dealing with it by making statements about it, authorizing views of it, describing it, by teaching it, settling it, ruling over it: in short, Orientalism as a Western style for dominating, restructuring, and having authority over the Orient."[8]

What Said offers as a definition of Orientalism is less a definition than an account of a particular and particularly momentous transubstantiation always immanent in the word for those of us who are in language. The "elaborate theories, epics, novels, social descriptions and political accounts" of Orientalism become the means and the models for "dominating, restructuring, and having authority over the Orient." Literary becomes political authority. A "style of thought" becomes a ruling order, an academic discipline a political regime.

Rule through the word brought immense resources against the minds and bodies of the colonized. Consider the *Requerimiento,* a document promulgated by the Spanish monarchy as a means for legitimating their colonial conquests in the Americas. The *Requerimiento* was to be read by Spanish officers on the occasions of their encounters with the peoples of the Americas. The document announced the Spanish monarchy's claim to lands in the New World, the warrant granted the monarchy by the Pope, the benefits offered to acquiescent inhabitants, and the violence they faced if they refused.[9] The *Requerimiento* answered the demands of visibility and publicity. The Indians might, if they wished, see "certain writings" in which the Pope conveyed title to the Spanish, and the officers were to take care to read the document in public. The *Requerimiento* also offered a rational justification for Spanish conquest, embedding it in a frame of scriptural citation and speculative world history. It surpasses Sade as an instance of the perverse authority of writing. This is the word as authority: compelling acquiescence. The *Requerimiento* invoked both a compelling rationality and the violence that stood before and behind it. The violence that stood with and within the *Requerimiento* made submission a rational necessity. The *Requerimiento* was not merely allied to and dependent upon violence: it contained violence, produced it, set it in motion.

Through these literary modes of rule, the colonizers transformed themselves. Those who remained in the metropole entered the colonies in literary form. They ruled through laws, policies, and regulations, in minutes and memoranda. They saw the results of their rule in writing and had the pleasures of dominion in the same form. Convinced, as many from Mill to Marx were, that their efforts brought the colonized into a progressive history formerly closed to them, "the Orientalist could celebrate his method, and his position, as that of a secular creator, a man who made new worlds as God had once made the old."[10] Those present in the colonies in the flesh were translated into a literary form that was both authoritative and unassailable. In this order, the empire was the word in the world, and the colonized were made flesh.

The colonized were made flesh, often wholly flesh, in a reading that went beyond racism in the ordinary sense. What made Africans different from other human beings, for Hannah Arendt, "was not at all the color of their skin but the fact that they behaved like a part of nature, that they treated nature as their undisputed master, that they had not created a human world."[11] Yet this curious separation from the human word and the human world seemed to inhere in the African skin, for it came with those enslaved bodies across the Middle Passage. For Arendt, the African American remained outside politics. The civil rights and black power movements belonged to the social, and addressed issues that were properly seen as outside politics. The only way for African Americans to enter the American polity was through a constitutional amendment mandating their inclusion. To become political, to become American, they would have to become written. Writing would overcome the flesh.

The problem, for the colonized Indians exported to Europe and Africans imported to America, was not, however, a dearth of language, or simple alienation from the word. The Indians had the *Requerimiento,* the slaves the documents that rendered them property. Both had become written.

Orientalism had the Enlightenment enthusiasm for taxonomy and classification. The "impulse to classify nature and man into types" had prepared the way for Orientalist structures.[12] These typologies were themselves transformed from physical descriptions to signifiers in moral and political systems. Racial and national types become signs of political and moral qualities ranged in a hierarchical system. The colonized, the Oriental, becomes not only an instance but a sign.

Albert Memmi's early and subtle study of the effects of colonization, *The Colonizer and the Colonized,* recognized the strategies of inversion in resistance that this transubstantiation set in motion. The colonized were variously subjected. Memmi wrote: "The middle class suffers most from bilingualism. The intellectual lives more in cultural anguish, and the illiterate person is simply walled into his language." In this prison house of language it is not, however, to the word but to the flesh that the colonized turns. "The first attempt of the colonized is to change his condition by changing his skin."[13] This was no misprision on the part of the colonized. Orientalism, and colonial authority within it, inscribed itself on the bodies of the colonized. They were transformed from mere beings to instances of a discourse, figures in the epics and social descriptions, novels and memoranda, of Orientalism. They had been not only inscribed in the Orientalist discourse but inscribed by it. They had become legible. They had been made to bear the texts of race.

An intimate and revelatory account of the reduction of the colonized to legible flesh ruled by the word is given by Frantz Fanon in *Black Skin, White Masks*. "Look, a Negro": Fanon hears the words from the mouth of a child, the least of the empire, yet still able to exercise the authority of the word. In that moment, in the imperial word, Fanon is made the object of the imperial gaze. He, the colonized subject, is wholly flesh, "a Negro." This body made Negro is the site as it is the sight of subjection. Fanon, in the recognition of subjection that would fuel colonial and postcolonial thought, seized this relation, turning the use of sight to theory, subjecting the authority of the word to exegesis. In becoming an author in the literary sense, he altered the structures of political authority. It was a strategy that would be often and successfully repeated.

Imperial rule had made the colonized Caliban, in a recurrent figure of postcolonial theory: "You taught me language; and my profit on't / Is, I know how to curse. The red plague rid you / For learning me your language."[14] Césaire, Senghor, Fanon, Kenyatta, and Cabral would do exactly that, and more. They seized the first weapon of the colonizer for their own. Nehru, writing, would give India the history denied it. Kenyatta, writing, would make custom the author of the future. Gandhi, writing, would craft a written self. Rushdie, writing, would claim literary authority and win imperial plaudits for that once-despised colonial patois.

Fanon writes in "The Negro and Language," "The problem we confront in this chapter is this: The Negro of the Antilles will be proportionately whiter—that is, he will come closer to being a real human being—in direct ratio to his mastery of the French language."[15] The problem of the confluence of political and literary authority, and of a system of colonization that rendered the colonized flesh alien to both, was, as Fanon recognized, the problem of the word written on the flesh. "The black man who has lived in France for a length of time returns radically changed. To express it in genetic terms, his phenotype undergoes a definitive, an absolute mutation."[16] He "becomes whiter."[17] The speech of the colonized, the "divine gurgling" of Creole, would write inferiority on the person of the immigrant colonized as authoritatively as a customs stamp. "Je suis Matiniquais, ce'st la pemie fois que je viens en Fance," declared Fanon's colonial arrival on his first visit to the metropole.[18] The elisions and omissions, the significant sounds of colonial speech, would betray him. Mothers, fathers, and schools taught the French of France, or the King's English. In the colonial order of the word and the flesh linguistic mastery did not simply raise one in the social order; it altered the flesh. It made one whiter.

For those who resisted colonial authority and the Orientalist discourse in which it resided, it was therefore necessary not only to gain linguistic mastery but to make it possible for the word to carry blackness as the sign of authority. This long process of mastery subversions, reclamation, and resistance offers a plethora of strategies. These strategies were often opposed to one another in practice and in principle but nevertheless advanced a common enterprise: the decolonization of linguistic authority. The Nehrus and Nirad Chaudhuri would make themselves master of the King's English. Senghor would seize the French of France and make it *nègre,* occupied by blackness. In Rushdie, the once-despised rhythms of colonial speech become the language of authority, yar. "Proper London, bhai! Here we come! Those bastards won't know what hit them. Meteor or lightning or vengeance of God. Out of thin air, baby. *Dharrraammm!* Wham, na? What an entrance, yaar."[19] Rushdie himself is altered by the process. As he writes, the speech of the colonized moves from the mouth to the hand, from characters to the author, from dialogue to narrative.[20]

In Rushdie, one sees that the word remains treacherous terrain for the postcolonial subject. "Here's a great lie, thinks the Grandee of Jahilia drifting into sleep: the pen is mightier than the sword."[21] Rushdie made himself an author, and authoritative, in the language of the empire. He made that language speak in the accents of the once-colonized. After the notorious fatwa, that authoritative writing, that made the author's body a target, Rushdie became the very icon of The Author. As an author, he was the sign of the universal and enlightened West; as an Easterner, his was the body subject to the power of the word. It was not only through Khomeini's fatwa that Rushdie was made vulnerable. The writing of the Western press and the pressure of Western writers likewise read Rushdie as "almost, but not quite" a Western author, still subject in the flesh to the power of the word, never quite its master. Rushdie became Saladin Chamcha, the man of many voices, adept of the logos, whose body betrays him.

Saladin Chamcha, formerly Salahuddin Chamchawala, leaves Mumbai (then Bombay) for England, where his imitative gift—"I have a gift for accents. Why shouldn't I employ?"—makes him a living and gives him a measure of discreet eminence. He is audible but not visible, and so not legible. He is "the man of a thousand voices." But in the wake of the air accident that tumbles Saladin Chamcha into an altered life, he loses control of his voices, finds himself speaking in the accents of the mother tongue he had abandoned, and inhabiting an altered body. "His thighs had grown uncommonly wide and powerful, as well as hairy. Below the knee the hairiness came to a halt and his legs narrowed into tough, bony, almost fleshless calves, terminating in a pair of shiny, cloven, hoofs, such as one might find on any billy-goat." He had become a goat, a devil, a satyr and a satire.[22]

Rushdie was subject to a similarly satiric transmutation. He has become the object lesson of Homi Bhabha's "Of Mimicry and Man." Almost but not quite a Western author, he is returned inexorably to his all too Eastern body. Almost but not quite master of writing, he is mastered by it, fallen from writer to the object of writing, the subject of the fatwa. Rushdie is caught in a web of uncertainties; the author of the fatwa dead, the regime alternately repealing and confirming the fatwa, knowing the penetrability of the West, uncertain of Western protection, subject to that "uncertainty, which fixes the colonial subject as a 'partial' presence."[23] Liberalism's promises betray themselves here. The promise to close the body and open the mind proves empty here, for the body remains at risk. The promise that writing offers a protective disembodiment, a means of secular transubstantiation, proves empty as well. Here writing is not protection but a double threat: writing (Rushdie's) makes the body vulnerable, and writing (Khomeini's) is the weapon aimed against it. In these myriad betrayals, liberalism betrays itself to itself. Bhabha writes, "The success of colonial appropriation depends on a proliferation of inappropriate objects that ensure its strategic failure, so that mimicry is at once resemblance and menace."[24] The desire of the West to take Rushdie in becomes the desire that took Rushdie in, a lie, perhaps, or merely wishful thinking. The liberal ambition to shelter the open mind in a body closed by the texts of the law and the power of the sovereign shows itself inadequate; shows, moreover, that writing is a weapon that can turn in the hand, and that the open mind can imperil the fragile body.

# 4
## Hand and Eye

---

$\lceil$ olonialism is the dominion of the eye. The eye that falls on the pho-
$\lfloor$ tograph, that reads a text, holds the body of the colonized within its
orbit. Word and flesh, law and territory fall under the governance of the
eye.

Europe saw a proliferation of visual representations of the colonized in Orientalist paintings, ethnographic treatises, and colonial
photography. Sight created site: the sight of empire became the site of
empire. The photographs themselves become the location of imperial
power. For the government, for readers of books, for visitors to
exhibits and museums, and for the private purchasers of postcards,
they were imperial possessions. These were the terrain on which power
was exercised.

Colonial photography is a practical performance that, like so many
others, anticipates theory. In it one sees the precession of the simulacrum, for in much of colonial photography the representation of
authority precedes its establishment. Here one can see the operation of
sight as power, the construction of the gaze as male. The peculiar contradictions of liberal empire are vividly on display here: the compulsory
character of rationality, universalism in the service of the particular,
democracy in the service of dominion.

The workings of the imperial hand and eye lay at the heart of
Barthes's account of semiotics in *Mythologies*. In this now canonical passage, Barthes moves from sight to power, from the quotidian to the
exotic, from commerce to politics, from literary ephemera to the structures of empire.

> I am at the barber's and a copy of *Paris-Match* is offered to me. On
> the cover, a young Negro in a French uniform is saluting, with his
> eyes uplifted, probably fixed on a fold of the tricolour. All this is the
> *meaning* of the picture. But, whether naively or not, I see very well
> what it signifies to me: the France is a great Empire, that all her sons,
> without any colour discrimination, serve under her flag, and that
> there is no better answer to the detractors of an alleged colonialism
> than the zeal shown by this Negro in the service of his so-called
> oppressors.[1]

Photography was then a medium that simultaneously denied and
asserted its own authority. The assertion "the camera never lies" was a
claim that the medium was transparent, neutral, and impotent, unable
to alter that which it brought before the eye. Yet this assertion of impotence was accompanied by a claim to offer access to the real: to pro-
nounce finally, truthfully, authoritatively. This curious transmutation
of denial into assertion is a peculiarly successful strategy characteristic
of the compulsory and coercive universalism of liberal imperialism.
Photography's claim to neutral representation enabled those it served
to pretend to objectivity even as the empire advanced particular interests. The transparency of the medium echoed the claims of coercive
rationality, compelling agreement, in a democratic disguise. Anyone
could see. Everyone, therefore, could see the facts that colonial photography laid before them. Everyone, therefore, must concur in a common, anticipated conclusion. In photography, as in the ideology of
liberal imperialism, the system of democratic representation was
enlisted in the service of dominion.

Colonial photography provided an ostensibly rational and hence
universal justification for empire. It also provided for the private, irrational, sensual enjoyment of empire. The democratic qualities of the
medium served dominion. Through the sense of sight, in the medium
of photography, the most impoverished and disenfranchised colonial
subject could enjoy his colonial possessions. He could gaze upon them,
marvel in their beauty, their terrors, their exoticism, and congratulate
himself on their possession. Photographs of landscapes and antiquities,
of monuments, edifices, and goods spread knowledge of the empire and
invested that knowledge with the pleasures of power. Sight gave an
attenuated access to the pleasures of dominion, knowledge carried
with it the consciousness of power. The techniques of photography
rendered the experience of empire more democratic, more mediated,
and more semiotic. They also enabled these eminently political plea-

sures to appear removed from politics, to present themselves in the guise of science or entertainment.

Photographic portraits of colonial landscapes and antiquities empty of people presented a *terra nullius* without prior claimants. The monuments or the land stood empty, and the imperial subject could look out upon his domains without hindrance, without temporal, geographic, or political constraints. Gazing on the landscape presented to him as his own, he could enter it unconscious of enmity and without anxiety, as if the land itself invited him in. As another settler colonist wrote, "The land was ours before we were the land's."[2]

In this solitary, domestic activity, the imperial project of penetration into the colonial interior was recapitulated photographically. The gazing imperial subject repeated—and reiterated—the nation's penetration into the territorial interior. He could enter freely not only into the land but into the houses of the colonized. He could pull aside the veil. Photography unveiled women of all classes, from the Begum of Bhopal to market women. The empire demanded portraits on passports. Newspapers circulated photographs of the poor in starving masses, the powerful on world tours. Academics and clinicians took, examined, and classified photographs of the colonized, naked and clothed, for ethnographic and medical projects. Through this work, and that of popular pornographers, the imperial subject's gaze could penetrate even into the bodies of the colonized.

The camera thus became the instrument of penetration into the colonial world, the privileged means for enjoying the possession of colonized people as well as colonized lands. In this visual economy, the colonized body is identified as the object of desire. The process of entry, penetration, and unveiling reveals more of the colonial mind than the colonized body, more of the word than the flesh. The photograph that invites the gaze is a visual interpellation, placing the—willing or unwilling, but inevitably complicit—eye in the site of empire. The private parts of politics are unveiled: political economy depends on a libidinal economy; the private is at the core of the political, and the claims of politics to isolate and conceal the private render it all too visible, all too public.

The process of progressive entry into the land, the houses, and the bodies of the colonized constructed the imperial viewer's gaze as male. The exclusion of the native, colonized male from the enjoyment of the object of desire was made explicit in the content of some (as in the form of all) these photographs. In figure 4-1, as in colonial photography alto-

Figure 4-1. Postcard "Young Moorish woman," p. 24 in Malek Alloula, *The Colonial Harem* (University of Minnesota Press, 1986).

gether, the colonized male is at once outside and inside. He is barred from the enjoyment of empire, and—anticipatorily, reassuringly— barred from entry into the domestic realm. The colonizer is able both to enter and to leave unconfined.

In these photographs the open Eastern body becomes the sign of the colonized Orient. Femininity, in this semiotic economy, marks subordination. The empire stood as husband and father, in nominal possession of the empire. The colony's identity was, like that of a daughter or a wife, erased under a common name. The colonial body, like the feminine body, was understood as open and penetrable. This has been observed often enough to have become a commonplace, but earliest and best in Said's description of the Orient's "feminine penetrability."[3] It is through this openness and penetrability that the empire subjects the colonized.

Orientalist art provides visual renderings of this inviting openness. These paintings, like Sade's texts, provide a vivid and erotic enactments of the contradictions of liberal dominion. Figure 4-2 recapitulates Western constructions of gendered bodies. The male body is closed. Every orifice is sealed, the head veiled, the mouth covered. This is the closed body that shelters the free will and the open mind. This is a body capable of possessing, but not open to possession. The eyes and the hands, the instruments of the logos, remain free. These instruments of the logos work here as the means to another's subjection. Hands and eyes reach into the woman's mouth. She stands open to the man's gaze, the man's hands. The feminine body is the body of the slave. She stands naked, unveiled, open to the man's sight, her body opened, penetrated, by his hand. The painting renders Eastern subjection as feminine and contrasts it with male closure, male mastery of the mouth, hand, and eye. The painting renders political domination as openness and penetrability of the body, as subjection to the gaze. Within the painting, the master's body is closed, free, and empowered.

A still greater mastery is given to the imperial hand and eye. Authority, in both senses, belongs to the hand that made the work. The imperial viewer subjects the native male as well as the woman. He too falls under the gaze of mastery as an object of desire, a commodity to be assessed. He is placed before the imperial gaze as an object of evaluation. The imperial viewer is called to judge the slave sale and the role of the seemingly powerful native male within it. Within the painting, the veiled man is a purchaser in the act of judgment, a master and holder of power. From the perspective of the viewer outside the painting, the

Figure 4-2. Jean-Léon Gérome, *Slave Market*, © Sterling and Francine Clark Art Institute, Williamstown, Massachusetts.

veiled man is a commodity whose worth is to be assessed, subject to moral evaluation of the viewer. His body too is on display, on the market; he too may be judged, he too may be owned. This ambivalent gendering of the Eastern male, masculine to women, feminine to Western men, reveals something of the signifying function of the veil, in this painting, and in Western representations of the East. The veil, which seems to deflect the gaze, attracts it. The veil, which seems to conceal otherness, draws the eye toward the sign of its absence. The veil, which seems to conceal and confine sexuality, marks the body as sexual. In Gérome's painting the veil on the Eastern man *attracts* the gaze, draws one's attention to the vulnerability of the body by marking its concealed openness. The ambiguity of the veil, which emphasizes that which it purports to conceal, conceals and reveals the ambiguity of the colonized man: at once despot and slave. Art echoes philosophy. The insistence on Oriental despotism that serves, in Hegel, in Marx, in Mill, as an apology for conquest of and dominion over the colonized, is here given visual, erotic, privately apprehended, form. The body of the colonized man is made an icon of dominion even as it is made subject to the gaze and opened to the desire of the colonizer.

Under colonial authority, men's bodies are rendered open, penetrable, subject—feminine—as well. Figure 4-3 is a painting of male bod-

Figure 4-3. Jean-Léon Gérome, *The Snake Charmer,* Sterling and Francine Clark Art Institute, Williamstown, Massachusetts; cover to Edward Said, *Orientalism* (New York: Random House 1978).

ies, is it not? Only men are present. There is, moreover, a conspicuous semiotic array of rifles, spears, and swords, as if Gérome insisted on the presence of the phallus. At the very center of the composition is a child's body, gendered male by a (very large) snake. All eyes are directed at the boy's loins, at the snake that serves as a phallus. This too would seem to be an icon of hypermasculinity. The boy's phallus is enlarged, animated. The gaze of the imperial viewer is, however, directed not at the phallus or its animal and mechanical avatars but at the boy's bottom, the site of penetration. These men, eminently male to each other, are presented to the imperial gaze as open, penetrable, and disarmed. The old man, servants, and soldiers have set their weapons aside or lean languidly upon them. The boy is subject to the gaze of the colonized powers (the old ruler, the armed men), but they are subject to the gaze of the imperial viewer. The colonized men confront, and are enthralled by, the sight of the phallus in their possession. The snake makes the phallus—animate, animal, disarming—visible to the imperial viewer, yet the boy's phallus, on which the gaze of the colonized men is fixed, remains invisible. The colonized body never shows itself to the imperial viewer as possessing the privileged sign of power.

The East, the Orient, is represented to the imperial viewer as a visual field of accessibility, and as a zone in which barriers between the sexes fall. In the East men (Eastern and Western, colonizer and colonized) have enhanced access to the bodies of women. The harem thus stood at the center of conceptions of the Orient, a zone of patriarchal power in which the commanding male might have not one but many women and enjoy the privilege of rule over castrated men. This was Richard Burton's "Sotadic Zone."[4] In this zone, male desire for possession and dominion was satisfied. Men would enjoy uninhibited access to the objects of desire. The imaginary constructions of the harem in the West made it an icon of more than heterosexual pleasure. In this zone, the bodies of men were also open and available.

The privileged position of the harem as the icon of the East served as both the justification for imperialism and the inducement to it. The confinement of women and the castration of men proved the Oriental despotism that liberal empire would combat. The defeat of that despotism tore down the walls that confined women, yet they were delivered not to themselves but to the enjoyment of the liberators. Liberal empire offered its adherents the pleasures of the dominion they prided themselves on opposing. Here too the open body served as sign for and evidence of the closed mind.

The open bodies of the colonized, of gay men and new women, posed the threat of inversion, sexual and political. The use of *inversion* as a term for homosexuality made homosexuality a metonym for all those instances in which the world turned upside down. The recognition of homosexuality raised the possibility that the most "natural" hierarchies could be overturned. It has raised other possibilities as well: anxiety about the subaltern, about subaltern studies, about the seductive open bodies of the colonized, about the seductions of cultural studies and postmodernism, about sexual openness, about political openness.

Visual representations of empire made the public private and the political erotic, and enlisted the libidinal economy in the advancement of the political economy. The privatization of empire in the visual (and the attendant eroticization of the political) removed the illicit private pleasures of political domination to a zone where they might remain discreetly concealed.

# 5
## Open Bodies, Closed Minds

Colonialism's demand that the colonized be seen, that they be accessible to the gaze of the colonizer, is answered by the refusal to be seen. In light of the colonial demand, the resurgence of veiling becomes a gesture denying access to the empire.

The desire to veil—or, more precisely, to deny the imperial gaze—is not the only response to postcoloniality. The imperative "you must be seen" is transformed from a command to a drive. The postcolonial order, which denies postcolonial significance on the world scene, impels them to make themselves visible, make themselves seen. Once the object of the empire's voyeuristic monopoly, they make themselves actors on the global stage. Once compelled to be seen by others, they are impelled to be seen by themselves. Once written of, written for, they become writers. Once made flesh, they come to make that flesh meaningful.

The idiom of postcoloniality focuses "above all, on the mouth, the belly, and the phallus," Achille Mbembe writes.[1] In the simplest sense, to eat is to take in, to become comprehensive, to grow, to enlarge, to increase. The colonized, once taken in, once held in another body politic, once diminished, now wish to grow, to enlarge, to increase, their own body politic. Food is a precious commodity in economies of scarcity. All commodities have, however, a double existence. Food not only satisfies a need, it carries meaning. In extravagant eating, food serves as both a metonymic and metaphoric sign. The presence of a great deal of food stands both for a great deal of goods of all sorts, and also for that which food signifies: nurture, comprehension, the resources for growth. The mouth is that which eats and commands.

The mouth as the site of speech, the engine of command, is replaced by the mouth as a source of pleasure and self-aggrandizement. The eye and the hand acquire renewed importance as signifiers of power. The eye is the iconic signifier of the drive to see oneself, to be seen, to see oneself seen. The hand holds. Those who cut off the hands of their enemies, or of those under their control, take the place of King Leopold. They become—however perversely—their own rulers. They enact the desire to prevent things from getting out of hand, the desire that others hand power over, the perversely literal response to the command "unhand them," and the desire to have the upper hand.

Colonialism was an act of penetration and occupation in which the empire entered and occupied the body of the colonized. These acts of penetration were indifferent to the will of the colonized but addressed the libidinal desires of the colonizers. The colonized body was the open body. In this semiotic economy, as in so many others, the phallus is the sign of power, the privileged sign of closure and self-possession. The colonized come to take power over the body politic for themselves, and when they do, the signifier of that power may acquire enhanced importance. In all of these drives, pleasure in the body replaces subjection in the body.

The semiotic economy of colonialism, in which the colonized body politic was the open body and the body subjected, places particular significance in orifices. Anticolonial anger and desire identify power with the closed body.

This is particularly the case with regard to the bodies of women. The discourses of empire, and indeed of the order of the word and the flesh in the metropole, read the colonized body as the body feminine: open to penetration, required to assume the name of the father, and to be absorbed, nominally, legally, into an encompassing body politic that would provide it closure. Anticolonial and postcolonial discourses have, like the imperial discourses to which they responded, given particular importance to the feminine. Nandy, Das, Kakar, Spivak, Stollar, and others have observed the dilemmas and conundrums that haunted anticolonialists determined to escape the subjecting binaries of semiotic gendering, and described the innovative tactics and strategies developed to overcome this discursive imprisonment. From the hypermasculinity of Subhas Chandra Bose to Gandhi's self-proclaimed and cleverly deployed femininity, from the revival of Sita and sati to Gayatri Spivak's reading of Devi's Draupadi, anticolonial discourses succeeded in undermining the determined reading of masculinity as power, femininity as subjection, with radical consequences for postcolonial subjectivity in the former metropole as well as the former colonies.

Three debates have, however, remained as artifacts of the sexed order governing the word and the flesh in a still colonized world. The debate over sati reaffirmed the construction, dear to liberal imperialists, of the Western man as liberator of Eastern women. The refusal to recognize feminine agency cast satis as presumptive victims of a culture still mired in custom. Western men (and now Western and Westernized women) presented themselves in this schema as enlightened liberators.

One of the favored gestures of the Enlightenment was tearing aside the veil. This gesture held an Aladdin's treasure of political references that would simultaneously enhance and subvert it. Behind the veil lay: what? A truth to be revealed or beauty to be possessed? What did the one who tore away the veil look for? Another's freedom, or his own pleasure? Tearing away the veil was an act that conflated liberator and violator, revealing liberalism's "forked tongue" in the work of the liberal hand and eye.[2] Enlightenment discourse had made the veil an ambivalent icon of oppression and seduction, promising more than moral satisfaction to those who tore away the veil.

The construction of the veil as the mark of the other, of oppression, of concealment and the preservation of an errant, alien way, made the veil a banner. Those who recognized the colonial and postcolonial economy of sight could take the veil as a denial of the male gaze, or of Western access. They could wear the veil as an affirmation of themselves as alien and other to the West, as the uniform of their allegiance to their own. The religious import of the veil only strengthened the force of the gesture.

Islam as the religion of the veil sits like Jerusalem at the crossroads of Western contradiction. Islam as Islam is the enemy of the Crusaders, the antithesis of European identity and Western religion. Islam as religion is, like all religion, the privileged enemy of the Enlightenment, the symbol of dark irrationality, the province of unreasoning superstition, oppressive hierarchies, and arbitrary rule. Opposition to Islam offers an illusory wholeness to a West divided. The embrace of Islam provided the means for a comprehensive rejection of the West and an oblique and satisfying recognition of Western contradictions. Memmi recognized this: "The colonized accepts and asserts himself with passion. But who is he? Surely not man in general, holder of universal values common to all men." This acquires still greater resonance for postcolonial women "excluded from that universality, both in word and in fact."[3] Religion offers not only an affirmation of (and for) the alien that is one's own against the universal, it is also "an extraordinary place of communion" covering the fissures of class and ideology. Memmi, seeing the power of "the old myths," saw that a new attention might "regenerate them dangerously."[4] The myths that were regenerated were twofold, and those of the West were no less hazardous than those of the East.

The third debate descended from the discourses of masculine and feminine, the closed body of power and the open body subjected, concerned the practice of sunnah, as it is called in Cairo, or female genital mutilation, as it is called in New York. (There are, of course, those in each city who prefer the other term.) The opponents of female genital mutilation argued that this was an instance of violence brought against women throughout the world, the survival of an earlier, less enlightened, and more patriarchal order. The defenders of sunnah argued that this practice enabled women to gain entry into the closed public spaces of the mosque, that governance of the bodies of women did not belong to the West, and that liberalism's claim to universal validity revealed itself here, and elsewhere, as unexamined parochialism. The debate rehearsed colonial debates in which control over the bodies of women became the semiotic and political occasion for contention over control of the body politic. Yet it departed from the traditional dichotomies. Much had already changed. The opponents of female genital mutilation argued for the openness of the female body to sexual pleasure and against the primacy of nationality, religion, or culture over gender. For the defenders of the practice, the opening of the woman's body became not the sign of subjection but a claim to political power and public presence.

All debates refused to recognize the legitimacy of the boundaries of decolonized states. All reaffirmed—and reenacted—the interventions (and the apologies for intervention) of the colonizing empires. None of the debates was, however, a triumph for liberal neoimperialism. In each case, the refusal to recognize boundaries and the legitimation of cross-cultural critique issued in a series of radical challenges to liberalism and the understanding of the feminine in the West.

The possession of a vast and conspicuous military apparatus closes the body politic as the veil closes the politicized body. Early anticolonialists, however, tended to seek not only (and not primarily) the closure furnished by well-armed militaries but the closure granted by autarchy. Postcolonials, rather than attempting to close off the open body, are driven to seek pleasure in the open body: to constitute the open body as a condition of pleasure and power. The desire to maintain boundaries and the armies that protect them, to erect protectionist barriers, and to veil are all manifest in postcolonial politics, but postcolonials may also be drawn to self-display, the black market, and the informal economy.

Colonialism—and persistent relations of economic dependency—made colonial and postcolonial states suppliers of natural resources and necessities to the metropole. The black market makes postcolonials the importers of luxuries brought in from the metropole. Extraction is replaced by imports. Deprivation is replaced by excess. The postcolonial economy strives semiotically as well as practically to replace the condition of not enough goods—or rights, or rule—with an excess of those objects of desire.

This discourse of power, like all others, is susceptible to irony, mockery, and carnivalesque subversion. Colonialism was the dominion of the word: the word of command, the word of classification, the word of constitution. Postcoloniality is a condition in which people have learned the power and the iridescence of words—and the bodies those words make. The meaning of eating and excess does not remain stable in the grand excesses of the banquets that mark not only official functions but the weddings and celebrations of the people. Mbembe writes,

> The obesity of men in power, their impressive physique, or, more crudely, the flow of shit which results from such a physique—these appeal to a people who can enjoy themselves with mockery and laughter, and, sometimes, even join in the feast.[5]

Food calls up shit as command calls up mockery. The acronym of the ruling party of Togo, RPT, "was identified with 'the sound of fecal matter dropping into a septic tank' " or "the sound of a fart emitted by quivering buttocks." Growth, enlargement, and increase can result in corruption, and the employment of a politically cathected and libidinally invested discourse—one that calls up both the pleasures of power and the pleasures of the body—offers no perfect protection to those in power. On the contrary: every claim to power calls up the critique of the nymph Echo, a discourse of resistance responsive to the claim. The more ordinary and pervasive the image that evokes power, the more easily it may be invested with an undermining egalitarianism.

> In this way an image such as the presidential anus is brought down to earth; it becomes nothing more than a common-or-garden arse that defecates like everyone else's. So too the penis of "His Excellency" turns out to be no more than a peasant's, unable to resist, amidst the aromas of everyday life, the scent of women.[6]

This bringing down to earth gives some confidence that the ordinary might slip out from under the weight of history. Here, in the entangling discourses of postcoloniality, is the vulgar, exuberant evidence for the embrace of openness on all sides, the presumption by the partisans of patriarchy and presidential authority and their carnivalesque critics alike of the ubiquity of the open body, and their common refusal to identify openness with simple subjection.

The vision of the closed body sheltering the open mind closed the minds of its partisans to the possibilities of bodies and politics differently constituted. Women's bodies were thought to be open by nature, men's bodies might be opened by willful perversity, and the bodies of the colonized might be opened by force, but all were thought to be subjected by openness. The postcolonial recognition of the possibilities still open to opened bodies, to the violated, the vulnerable, and the willfully open, answers the vision of an open mind in a closed body with a recognition of the pleasure and pain, danger and delights of openness. This more critical and comprehensive vision has a revolutionary genealogy.

# Section 2

# 6
## Writing over Blood

---

The British remember the Glorious Revolution as the victory of the rule of the law over the body of the king, of a scriptural Protestantism over an all too fleshy Catholicism: as the victory of writing over blood.[1] For Trevelyan, the Glorious Revolution was "an agreed contract," concluded in that moment in Whitehall when William accepts the Declaration of Rights and Parliament acknowledges him as king.[2] The remembered history of the Glorious Revolution is a chain of literary transubstantiations; repeatedly, flesh becomes word. At each moment when blood—bloodshed or blood ties—should decide the issue, the word intervenes. Armies were amassed and concealed, allies readied, an invasion launched, a king deposed, a conquering king enthroned. Yet more ink than blood was spilled in this revolution. The execution of James II was forgone in favor of an Instrument of Abdication. William acquired title to sovereignty not through acts of war but through an act of Parliament.

William came to England with an army of invasion, but he came by invitation. Invasions by invitation are a commonplace now. They were an innovation then. William insisted not on the provision of arms (though he expected these to follow), but upon a letter signed by men of consequence in England assuring him of their support. They signed in cipher. He sailed armed with a text.

Contemporary paintings portray a very literary landing. The ships that landed at Torbay flew banners with "Pro religione protestante," "Pro libertate et religione," and "Pro libero parliamento" appended to the Orange motto "Je maintiendrai." The banners were not the archaic and ornamental emblems of a lineage; they announced positions in a present controversy. The words written on the banners were not mere ornaments. They were to be read.

The landing in England was immediately followed not by the bloodshed of earlier invasions but by the reading and publication of William's Declaration. The detailed account of the wrongs committed by the reigning monarch, the invitation to a rebellion in defense of rights, would find fuller expression in a later Declaration that likewise appealed to the judgment of "a candid world." James's original title to rule goes unchallenged; it is his conduct that is indicted. William's Declaration is witness to an ethic of responsibility. This doubly scriptural force, Protestant and literary, brought with it both the Protestant ethic and the spirit of capitalism. The invasion answered the call for an accounting.

The campaign that followed was conducted not through arms but through writing. William brought a printing press along with more traditional armaments, and this proved the decisive weapon of the war. The press was a formidable force in the Netherlands, operating on Dutch politics and providing a means for refugees, dissidents, and the States to influence affairs throughout Europe. William was accustomed to its use in the Netherlands and as a means for protecting an interest in the British succession. Copies of William's Declaration, two gazettes a week, pamphlets, tracts, and copies of correspondence between England and France were printed and circulated actively throughout England and Scotland.[3] James responded, and a legion of independent agents enlisted themselves in the controversy.

This campaign in print did not leave the body untouched. In the histories of the Glorious Revolution, the authority of Parliament is called forth by a barren womb. For some years, Mary of Modena's womb had held nothing but Protestant hopes. When she gave birth to a son, those hopes proved more than equal to the challenge. Words undid the succession the body had secured. The presence of the child's body was answered with rumors that placed the birth in doubt. The new Prince of Wales was declared a supposititious child, smuggled into the bedroom and the succession in a warming pan.

The warming-pan scandal holds the seed of the Glorious Revolution within it. James, insisting upon the claims of the body, accedes unconsciously to the power of the word, supplying an assembly of lords spiritual and temporal with a comprehensive and intimate array of gynecological testimony. Interested parties interrogated midwives and laundresses, interpreted the evidence, and published conflicting accounts of the evidence. The proliferation of debate invited the people to sit in judgment on the body's title. Even those of the blood royal assumed the need for a popular accounting. Anne wrote to Mary, "It may be it is our brother, but God only knows, for she never took care to satisfy the world, or give people any demonstration of it."[4]

There was, of course, a good deal of evidence for the child's birth. The child was born and the navel string cut in the presence of witnesses. The evidence of delivery was seen on the linen; milk was seen on the queen's breasts.[5] Physical evidence however, was not sufficient to counter the power of the word. The word, and the wind in the word, would bring more powerful forces. "Rock-a-bye baby in the tree tops, / When the wind blows the cradle will rock./ When the bough breaks, the cradle will fall, / And down will come baby, cradle, and all." Legitimate or changeling, the baby was to be no match for the Protestant wind.

William, for one, appears never to have doubted the child's legitimacy, though he came, prudently, to keep that opinion to himself. He included provisions concerning the supposititious birth in the Declaration on the insistence of the British who held them essential (he did not) only after extended consultations with his Dutch advisers, and gave the matter rather short shrift.

William knew well how fragile the claims of the body could be. Born to the hereditary office of Stadholder, he had already seen it denied to the House of Nassau (by an only nominally Perpetual Edict) and restored. His maternal grandfather had been beheaded, his uncles exiled—and, restored. William had no reason to have faith in titles that were written in the blood. Instructed by experience that hereditary claims could be set aside by the demands of time or policy, the stadholder was inclined to dwell on failures of performance.

William's history is that of stadholder, statesman, and Child of State. He was the posthumous child of the old order, raised by the republic. He was born posthumously to Mary Stuart, widow of William II, a stadholder with distinctly regal pretensions. The child William's upbringing was the subject of considerable debate, controversy, and amendment. In 1666 he was declared the "Child of State" and placed in the care (and under the surveillance) of Johan de Witt, the raadpensionary, a republican statesman who was the unequivocal enemy of the stadholderate and the House of Orange. His godfathers had been the regents of the republic, his christening present a letter of credit. Considerations of blood and a romantic (if not a desperate) conception of the stadholder as the hereditary defender of the Netherlands led to William's accession.[6] Yet though the Perpetual Edict was rescinded, it remained present to the minds of William and his compatriots. William's claim to the stadholderate was one of blood, but he came to the office by election and vindicated his claim by performance. He held it as an office, with prescribed responsibilities, duties, and limits. He was held (and he would hold himself) accountable. His success as stadholder, and in forging the European alliance, was secured by diplomacy.

Histories, obscurely conscious of the orders that confront one another in the enmity of William of Orange and Louis XIV, have made Louis fond of war and the pageantry of war, a victorious king seconded by superb generals. William has been made the architect of European unity, whose victories were won less by arms than by diplomacy. Louis's wars comprise battles, sieges, astonishing defeats, expected victories, and Te Deums—wars in which royal cousins corresponded across the lines of enmity, and strategic pursuits might give way to the need for celebratory ceremonials. William's wars are modern: wars of preparation and waiting, of rallying resistant populations and stemming desertions, wars of logistics and negotiation—wars in which fellow countrymen prepare, in William's words, to "die in the last ditch." The truth of the ideal masks empirical truths here. William's forces had their victories (upon which their survival depended) and their Te Deums. The officers, with relatives and friends in the enemy camp, corresponded and exchanged small luxuries across the lines. William's conduct accorded to an ancient model of private courage and public risk. It was Louis who advanced the formation of a protobureaucratic French state, and Louis who preferred to plan at home rather than risk bodily harm at war. It was William of whom it was said "in battle he is all fire." Conde, perhaps the greatest general of his time, reported to Louis that "the Prince of Orange has acted in all respects like an old captain, except in venturing his life too much, like a young one."[7] Laurence Sterne's thoroughly irreverent *Tristram Shandy* captures the regard in which William's soldiers held him.

Nevertheless, the obscure consensus that has commonly dismissed these facts as insignificant is not in error. The traditions (and traditional histories) that dismiss William's archaic valor for his modern nationalism, that see Louis winning in blood and losing in writing, rightly see an end and a beginning immanent in their wars. Macaulay, chronicling William's bravery at Landen, marks this not as a vestige of archaic bravery but as the work of modern rationality.

Never, perhaps, was the change which the progress of civilization has produced in the art of war more strikingly illustrated than on that day. . . . At Landen two poor sickly beings, who, in a rude state of society would have been regarded as too puny to bear any part in combats, were the souls of two great armies. In some heathen countries they would have been exposed at birth. In Christendom they would, six hundred years earlier, have been sent to some quiet cloister. But their lot had fallen on a time when men had discovered that strength of the muscles is far inferior to the strength of the mind.[8]

The English, watching the march of William's force through England, could have read the arrival of a new order in its structure. The invading army was disciplined and orderly, governed by the conceptions of office and accountability that animated William's Declaration.[9] Two of the casualties of the invasion would be furnished by William from his own troops—he had them hanged for looting. James would be astonished to discover Catholics among the soldiers guarding his captivity. When he remarked on this to an officer, he received the most Weberian of replies: "Yes, but we have Protestant swords."[10]

The defeat of James is accomplished without battle, almost without bloodshed. James pauses in his flight to exile, not to raise an army, but to throw a more literary obstacle in William's way: he casts the Great Seal into the Thames. There could be no more meaningful concession to the order that defeated James than this small act, intended to impede its triumph. In it James acknowledges the power of the word to rule. Though James is captured, and (incompetence in flight) captured again, he is not killed. William goes to great lengths to prevent the shedding of James Stuart's blood and finally succeeds at providing him with a sufficiently simple means of escape. Though James in the flesh still claims the throne, he is declared to have abdicated by an act of Parliament. A poem of the period recognized the confrontation of word and flesh in the claims of James and William. James argues

> Nature here pleads; your blood is on my side
> Each beating pulse and every vein allied.

William answers

> Titles to crowns from civil contracts spring.
> And he who breaks the law dissolves the king.[11]

After James, Mary Stuart stood, by right of blood, next in line to the throne. William was reluctant to serve as her consort, however, and

Mary declined to displace him. Burnet writes that it was he who acquainted Mary Stuart with the superior title she had in the body. He had asked her "what she intended the prince should be, if she came to the crown." The princess of Orange "did not understand my meaning, but fancied that whatever accrued to her would likewise accrue to him in the right of marriage." She had assumed both the authority of writing over the authority of the body, and with it the authority of men over women. When Burnet had instructed her that "it was not so," Mary affirmed, before William, what she had previously assumed, citing her submission to scripture: "Wives be obedient to your husbands in all things."[12] In this history, William owes the crown not to conquest, not to bloodlines or bloodshed, but to a member of the clergy, a reading of scripture, a marriage contract, and Mary's word. He could have had no more Weberian investiture.

The ascendancy of performance over bloodlines and the attendant ethic of responsibility emerge again in the terms of the settlement. James is held accountable for violations and infringements of these rights. The accession of William and Mary is made to depend upon their acceptance of constraints upon their rule.

The line of succession after them is determined by scripture as well. Mary is barren, Anne's children die. Much of the resonance of these phrases is lost to our day. Anne is, to Catholics and the Church of England, the patron saint of motherhood, the mother of Mary the Mother of God. The failing of Anne's maternity, the barrenness of the womb of Mary, the insistence on the barrenness of Mary of Modena, prefigure the evasion of incarnation. In this history, the power of the word does not depend upon the flesh. Familial yields to legislative authority. The line of succession is settled in an act of Parliament, adherence to the Protestant faith is mandated. Where the body has failed, the word succeeds.

# 7
## The Man of Blood and the Army of Scripture

British historians found this triumph of the word over blood the defining glory of the English. Trevelyan wrote, "It is England's true glory that the cataclysm of James's overthrow was not accompanied by the shedding of English blood either on the field or on the scaffold." He praises William's "brief and bloodless campaign" and compares the revolution, as Burke did, to that in France. "Here, seen at long range is 'glory,' burning steadily for 250 years: it is not the fierce, short, destructive blaze of *la gloire*."[1]

This revolution, "drawn up by great lawyers and wise statesmen," was, however, preceded by another, in which the Army of Scripture met the Man of Blood in battle: a revolution consummated by the death of the king.[2] The beginnings of the Glorious Revolution "were, like the beginnings of everything great on earth, soaked in blood thoroughly, and for a long time."[3]

Charles Stuart laid claim to a title written in the blood. Divine right passed, in his view, through the generations from one monarch to the next. England, he would declare at his trial, was "an hereditary Kingdom for near these thousand years." According to Charles, "a subject and a sovereign are clean different things."[4] The title that blood carried between the generations conferred an absolute authority. Charles Stuart had supported that claim by bloodshed.

He had his first foe in the Parliamentary Army, the second in the Army's Parliament. Each showed the lineaments of a nascent rational legal order. John Pym, whom a colleague would call "director of the whole machine," figures in these accounts as a minor bureaucratic demiurge. He had organized and, perhaps more importantly, continued to supply, an army in the field. He adapted the excise system developed by the Dutch. He developed a committee system in the shires, linked to an expanded and rationalized central administration.[5]

The New Model Army opposed itself not only to the principles of the Royalist force but to its organization. One advanced through merit and performance. The army, despite (or rather, because of) its intense appetite for preaching and prophecy, did not insist on uniformity of belief. "The State in choosing men to serve it takes no notice of their opinion: if they be willing faithfully to serve it, that satisfies."[6] A nascent sense of the separation of person and office, public duty and private belief, ordered the army.

Carlyle saw the civil war as a confrontation of the conflicting principles of word and flesh, but not in the form of a conflict between king and Parliament, or monarchy and the rule of law. In Carlyle's account the principle of kingship becomes a matter of mind rather than body. The proper king is identified through his relation to an etymology rather than a genealogy. Words rather than blood become the primary determinants of kingship. Words alone do not suffice for Carlyle. The word must become flesh. Men must surrender to the rule of scripture, and scripture must become embodied in the world through the labor of men.

Parliament recedes in Carlyle's history. The army steps forward. Parliament represents, for Carlyle, not only the impotence of words alone but the hazards of anarchy and aporia. In Parliament, among the republicans, Ranters and Levellers, royalists and Fifth Monarchists, "conflicting and colliding elements" meet, but cannot be united or made uniform.[7] They can accomplish no certain or lasting work. In the army Carlyle sees not words, but the power of the word. Here logos shows itself as law, commanding and authoritative. In Carlyle's history, it is as scripture that the word makes itself real in the world.

Carlyle located the seed of the New Model Army in Cromwell's belief that "to cope with men of honour we must have men of religion."[8] One principle must be answered with another, stronger. In this Cromwellian opposition, breeding is to be answered with discipline, blood with scripture.

For Carlyle, the Puritans were the force of "Heroism and Veracity," "Thought and Manhood." Cromwell's sword was merely an instrument. Cromwell's status as Lord Protector was thus ascribed by Carlyle—as it had been by Cromwell—to providence. The army was likewise subordinated, first to Parliament and the law, later to the unanswerable commands of scripture and necessity. Cromwell reports to the Parliament of "your Army." His later letters suggest the Army came to answer to a higher authority. "It would do you good," he writes, "to see and hear our poor foot go up and down making their boast of God."[9] "Your Army" had become "ours," and that "ours" had become little more than a courtesy, since the Army had refused the orders of Parliament to disband. The Army, which once was the arm of Parliament, had become its ruler, editing its membership under Colonel Pride, drawing close to London when the workings of Parliament displeased it. When it met in conclave in defiance of Parliament, Carlyle saw it not as a refusal of order but as order's incarnation. This was not an army in rebellion against civilian government, but "Army Parliament . . . against Civil Parliament": "An Armed Parliament, extra-official, yet not without a kind of sacredness, and an Oliver Cromwell at the head of it; demanding with one voice, as deep as ever spake in England, 'Justice, Justice!' under the vault of Heaven."[10] This army spoke "with one voice." Particular men who distinguished themselves in battle "look not to be named." Cromwell writes to Parliament, "We that serve you beg of you not to own us, —but God alone" and exhorts them to "disown yourselves; —but own your Authority."[11]

If the army was outside the law, it nevertheless demanded "'Justice, Justice!' under the vault of Heaven." Parliament acted for the people of England. The army acted for God. This was an army that thought itself the hand of providence, whose commands could not be evaded. When the purged members of Parliament, "asking By what Law? and ever again, By what Law?" directed their question to Hugh Peters, he would answer, "It is by the Law of Necessity; truly, by the Power of the Sword."[12]

Cromwell, with the bluntness that commanded Freud's admiration, stated the case more clearly. He would justify his actions on the ground not of law but of necessity. "The ground of Necessity, for justifying of men's actions is above all considerations of instituted Law; and if this or any other State should go about, —as I know they never will—, to make Laws against Events . . . then I think they will be making Laws against Providence."[13] For Carlyle's Puritans, scripture was the realm of command. Right reason, to men persuaded of the truth of scripture and their enlightened apprehension of the will of God, led inexorably to obedience. Rationality appears, to Carlyle's Puritans, not as the realm of an aporetic reason, always open, always questioning, but as merely a means to the recognition of, and submission to, the commands of providence. Acquiescence to necessity could thus be understood as submission to the commands of God. Parliaments debated, but where their debate stayed the hand of an army already in the hand of providence, Cromwell scorned them. Puritan England was to be the instrument and the imitation of providence. "Words! Truly our business is to speak Things."[14]

The verdict of philosophy was of no concern to Carlyle: "owls and godless men who hate the lightning and the light, and love the mephitic dusk and darkness, are no judges of the actions of heroes!"[15] In Carlyle's curious condemnation, Hegel is simultaneously appropriated, distorted, and condemned. Enlightenment belongs to the forces of Scripture and godly men, but these are no longer philosophers. When the owl of Minerva takes flight, in Carlyle's account, it is as a creature of darkness, one that makes waste.

Rationality, the order of the word, was to be secured not by the many, an anarchic people given license by equality, or by the "conflicting and colliding elements" of Parliament, but by the Canning Man. "Clearly enough to them, and to us, there can only one thing be done: search be made Whether there is any King, Konning, Canning, or Supremely Able-Man that you can fall-in with, to take charge of these conflicting and colliding elements, drifting toward swift wreck otherwise."[16] For Cromwell, as for Hegel, the unity of the state found not only expression, but active realization in the person of the king. "Puritanism, without its king is kingless, anarchic."[17] This was no endorsement of title in the blood or the power of the flesh. On the contrary, rule of the Single Person was thought essential because it conferred upon the state single-mindedness: unity of will.

The Canning Man replaced the Man of Blood. Yet Carlyle does not disguise Cromwell's use of the army, or the violence of the civil wars. In his account the change from the authority of blood to that of canning, altered its constitution. "Shedders of blood?" he asks. "Yes, blood is occasionally shed. The healing Surgeon, the sacrificial Priest, the august Judge, pronouncer of god's oracles to men, these and the atrocious murderer are alike shedders of blood; and it is an owl's eye that, except for the dresses they wear, discerns no difference."[18]

The New Model Army was an entity altered not only in its organization, but in its essence. Bloodshed was merely incidental. The army had become an armed Parliament and an army of scripture, advanced not by bloodshed but by the success of the word in the world. They were doing the work of surgeon and priest, prophet and judge. They were men of their word. This was to be a "Government of Heroism and Veracity" or, at worst, "the endeavor after Heroism and Veracity."[19] Making the revealed truth real in the world was the project of heroes in the service of veracity. Carlyle insists upon the continuing presence of these truths made material. "The works of a man, bury them under what guano-mountains and obscene owl-droppings you will, do not perish, cannot perish."[20] Carlyle's philosophers and scholars belong to the same species as Burke's Jacobins.

Carlyle thought the Good Old Cause "great, manlike, fruitful to all generations."[21] The army of scripture was an army of thought and manhood, with a voice "as deep as ever spake in England." The voices he heard were "The Voices of our Fathers."[22] They had become "Heroic" and "manlike" because scriptural morality had "bodied itself forth" for—and in—them.[23] For Carlyle, as for the engraver of the *Eikon Basilike,* the word became flesh through the labor of men.

Carlyle writes, "The Trial of Charles Stuart falls not to be described in this place; the deep meanings that lie in it cannot be so much as glanced at here." Carlyle has his own mystery of transubstantiation. The section is entitled "Death-warrant." Regicide figures in Carlyle's account as a matter of words, not blood. He records Bradshaw's affirmation of the court's authority, the command "Clerk, read the sentence!" and gives in full the text of "the Document" that was to serve as the warrant for Charles Stuart's execution. It is only in the words of this text that the execution, not yet accomplished, figures at all. Carlyle subordinates the king's blood to the words of this "stern Document . . . not specifically of Oliver's composition, but expressing in every letter of it the conviction of Oliver's heart."[24]

For others, Freud among them, the will to power, the disdain for title in the blood, and a firm belief in the impermanence of the flesh proved themselves in regicide. The execution of the first Charles Stuart was to be not the death of a man but the death of a king. He was named as king in the charge, before the court, in the warrant for his execution, and on the scaffold. This death would put an end to the idolatry of the flesh. Cromwell acknowledged no sanctity in the king's body: "I will cut off his head with the crown on it," he told Algernon Sidney. So said the regicide John Cook: "He must die and monarchy must die with him."[25]

The king died, but monarchy did not die with him. The Restoration demanded that several of the regicides answer for their signatures with their blood. Thomas Harrison gave a clear accounting. He had told the king that the actions of army and Parliament would be "open to the eyes of the world." He told the court that would sentence him to death, "I do not come to be denying anything, but rather to be bringing it forth to the light. . . . It was not a thing done in a corner. I believe the sound of it hath been in most nations."[26] Harrison's willingness to testify stands in sharp contrast to the manner of the king at his trial. Charles Stuart had refused to plead or give an account of himself before the court. Harrison would give an account of himself as readily before a court whose authority he disdained as he would give it before the nations. Testimony was a scriptural obligation. Yet Harrison had not entirely lost faith in the power of blood. When an onlooker at his execution called out the mocking question "Where is your Good Old Cause now?" Harrison answered, "Here in my bosom and I shall seal it with my blood."[27]

The regicides did not lose their faith in blood or accomplish the ending of the monarchy, but the forces of scripture had an enduring victory nevertheless. Nowhere is that victory more apparent than in the writing of the royalists. With the consummation of Cromwell's regicide Charles Stuart became Charles the Martyr. The forms in which this transcendence was recorded bear witness to the depth and finality of the victory of scripture over blood. The text and the allegorical frontispiece to the *Eikon Basilike* reveal the terms of Charles Stuart's redemption and transcendence (figure 7-1).

The frontispiece to *Eikon Basilike* is a portrait not of Charles Stuart nor of a dying king but of an Annunciation. This is the frontispiece to a new testament. Charles Stuart kneels, like Mary, before the text, a text inscribed "In tuo verbo spes mea." Like Mary, his body is open to the Holy Spirit; words enter him. He conceives, however, not the word incarnate but a vision of glorious disembodiment. The body is to be left behind. This is the transubstantiation not of word to flesh but of flesh to word.

Charles is shown in the act of conception, but it is himself he conceives, in another form. He takes on the attributes of Christ, the crown of thorns in this world, a crown of "beatam et aeternam gloria" in the next. In collapsing the submission of Mary and the submission of Jesus, the Annunciation, and the Crucifixion, the icon leaves the body behind, and erases the feminine. Charles conceives through the mind and the

Figure 7-1. Frontispiece to *Eikon Basilike Eikon Basilike: the Pourtraicture of His Sacred Majestie in His Solitudes and Sufferings,* facsimile of the 1648 edition (London: Elliot Stock, 1880), 6.

mind's eye. His conception issues not in the incarnate word but in a vision of unworldly glory. The feminine, and the body, have been effaced.

In the *Eikon Basilike,* as in the emblems of the French and American republics, power comes through the eye. Yet though the king is shown seeing, in the text and in the frontispiece Charles Stuart is opened to the eye of the people. The text casts the reader as confessor, judge, witness, and voyeur. The king confesses his "sinful frailty" in the earl of Strafford's death:

> I was persuaded . . . to choose rather what was safe than what seemed just. So far am I from excusing or denying that compliance on my part (for plenary consent it was not) to his destruction whom in my judgement I thought not, by any clear law, guilty of death, that I

never bare any touch of conscience with greater regret; which, as a sign of my repentance, I have often with sorrow confessed both to God and men.[28]

This text is testament to a new covenant. In it a man of letters takes the place of the king. The people, looking into the king's inmost heart, watching and judging, are put in the place of god. All, king and commoners, come under surveillance. All are called to account.

The same drama of judgment is recalled in Paul Delaroche's *Cromwell Gazing at the Body of Charles I* (figure 7-2). In this portrait, painted in 1831 on the eve of another moment in the liberal revolutions, Cromwell looks down upon a dead man. There are no signs of Charles Stuart's rank. He lies in a coffin, dead, as all men die. His body lies opened by the axe of the executioner, open to the gaze of Cromwell, open to the eye of the viewer. Cromwell's gesture, opening the coffin, permits the people to look upon the open body of the king. The composition brings Oliver Cromwell and Charles Stuart before our eyes. Here, as in the *Eikon Basilike,* the watching people are called upon to sit in judgment on the dead. People would continue to place this past before the eyes of posterity. William Frederick Yeames's composition *And When Did You Last See Your Father?* (figure 7-3), painted more than

Figure 7-2. "Cromwell Gazing at the Body of Charles I" Paul Delaroche, Musee des Beaux Arts, Nimes.

Figure 7-3. William Frederick Yeames, *"And When Did You Last See Your Father?,"* Walker Art Gallery, Liverpool, 1878 from Strong.

two centuries later, is anecdotal rather than allegorical, domestic rather than hagiographic. Yet this painting, no less than the *Eikon Basilike,* testifies to the power of the word and the ascendancy of the closed masculine body. The painting ranges Puritan against Cavalier. The Puritans are marked as the forces of scripture in the broadest sense, sitting at a table, papers before them. One speaks, one writes. One, blocking a doorway, holds a closed chest. At the opposite end of the composition, before the women, a larger chest stands open. The open and the closed, female and male, mark the poles of the composition. The Puritans are all men, the Royalists all women; the male child standing between them is the question at the center of the composition. The family is endangered by the word, the Puritans empowered. This painting opens the past, a moment, a household, before us. Yet it marks openness, the opened household, the open mouth of the answering child, as the site of danger. Here, as in the more graphic portraits of the French Revolution, the open body is associated with danger, with death. Whether one stands with the Royalists or sits with the Puritans, there is danger in the house.

The same transformation of the household, from a closed place of security to a site of danger, is written into portraits of the Stuarts. In the dynastic decline of the Stuarts, as in the broader realm of social relations, historians have recognized the transformation of family politics into the politics of the family. The first Charles Stuart figures as the exemplar of patriarchal authority. Goodall's *An Episode of the Happier Days of Charles*

*I* shows exactly that, with Charles Stuart as patriarch, dominant and benign. Daniel Maclise's *An Interview between Charles I and Oliver Cromwell* (figure 7-4) places Cromwell at one end of a table, Charles, children, and dogs at the other. Two forms of authority, two shapes of life, two epochs are opposed here. Charles, sitting in a pool of light, is turned toward the reader, his arms spread in a loose embrace, one arm encircling his son. His daughter leans against one knee; a greyhound affectionately rests its chin on the other. Cromwell, armed, sits half in shadow. Behind him, in deeper shadow, are two men, one armed, one writing. The loose, indulgent authority of the family is confronted here by military discipline and scriptural authority.

The first Charles Stuart signified the family safely united under patriarchal authority. The second Charles Stuart came to signify the patriarchal family in decay. *Charles II's Last Sunday* shows the king with several women, none his wife, among basset-playing Sabbath violaters, all engaged in similarly frivolous pursuits. For more literary commentators as well, Evelyn and Pepys, the second Charles Stuart and his brother James signified not the benevolent and unifying patriarchy of Filmer but the hazards of aristocratic sexuality. The second Charles Stuart's ennobled mistresses and illegitimate offspring suggested an aristocracy

Figure 7-4. Daniel Maclise, *An Interview between Charles I and Oliver Cromwell*, 1836, National Gallery of Ireland, Dublin, from Strong.

founded upon open bodies and extending itself through corruption. The rebellion of Monmouth suggested that the monarch's unrestrained sexuality had begotten treason. James Stuart also exemplified a corrupt and hazardous sexuality. The ever-extending, diseased body of the fat and promiscuous Ann Hyde was an image of appetite and corruption. The beautiful Mary of Modena, the "Daughter of the Pope," was an image of seductive Catholicism, the threat of a more potent treason. James Stuart's success in begetting a son would endanger the nation. Under this generation of Stuarts, the lines of descent from father to son signified not the traditional unity and continuance of the kingdom but treason and national dissolution.

William and Mary were, however, separated from the traditional order of the Stuart family. William's father died before his birth. His mother, invested with only a partial and divided authority, died during his childhood. His relations with his Stuart uncles had been marked by theft, manipulation, deception, and betrayal. William had, however, a passionate loyalty to his friends and to his nation. This preference for relations of affinity rather than those of family confounded the calculations of Louis XIV and Charles II. After William's visit to England in 1671, the French ambassador to England, Colbert de Croissy, reported to Louis that Charles had found his nephew William "so passionate a Dutchman" that he could not be entrusted with knowledge of their plans for his own dynastic advancement. English anxiety—and monarchical puzzlement—over William's friendships and Dutch nationalism signal the uneasy advent of an order where familial relations might take second place to the consuming passions of nationalism. The construction of William as a man who systematically advanced the cause of European Protestantism against the ambitions of Louis XIV recognizes in him qualities alien to a traditional prince. In his indifference to dynastic interests, his passionate advancement of interests of the state, William as stadholder emerges as an exemplar of politics as a vocation.

Mary was also separated from her lineage. Mary's rejection of her father for her husband is essential to the meaning—as it was to the success—of the Glorious Revolution. Her withdrawal of loyalty from her father removed the imminent danger present in James's patriarchal authority, but it raised the specter of the Medusa. Jacobite sympathizers would portray Mary entering Whitehall as the market women would enter the Tuileries, laughing and looking in the drawers. She was castigated as "a Tullia," bent on parricide and power.

> Thou wouldst, like Tullia, with triumphant pride
> Thy chariot drive, winged with ambitious fire
> O'er the dead body of thy mangled sire.[29]

These were answered with the explanation that in her demeanor, as in all things, she had merely obeyed her husband.

> I took the liberty to ask her, how it came that what she saw in so sad a revolution, as to her father's person had not made a greater impression on her. . . . And she assured me, she felt the sense of it very lively upon her thoughts. But she told me, that the letters which had been writ to her, had obliged her to put on a cheerfulness, in which she might perhaps go too far, because she was obeying directions, and acting a part which was not very natural to her.[30]

Obedience to scriptural authority (William's as well as God's) obliged Mary to exchange the instincts of a child of the flesh for the duties of a rational actor. Duty to private contracts and the public welfare—her official duties and an emerging rational legal order—required her to "act a part." The "natural" sentiments of the daughter yielded to the obedience of the wife.

Images of wifely devotion dominate biographic accounts of Mary, from Burnet to the present. From her charming and effusive childhood letters to her "dear crual loved blest husban" Frances Apsley to her empowering of William—"I am sorry I have but three crowns to give him"—Mary is "your loving obedient wife." Whether she is seen as an infant Sappho or an exemplar of "family values," Mary is hailed by the discourse of companionate marriage. For women in this discourse, submission becomes the necessary gesture of love. Thus Mary, writing to Frances Apsley, signs herself "your dog in a string your fish in a net your bird in a cage your humbel trout."[31]

Mary's submission to William was legible in both the terms of the settlement and the ceremonies marking it. The settlement invested William with administrative powers for his lifetime. At the ceremony in which the Declaration of Rights was presented, William and Mary entered and sat enthroned before the convention, hand in hand, as one body.[32] After the reading of the Declaration of Rights, William accepted the crown (and the declaration) for them both.

The specter of feminine power faded with Mary's submission. She had refused not obedience but obedience to her father. She set aside lineage for contract, blood for words. She refused to claim the throne for herself, according to the title she held in her body—a title independent of (and superior to) William's. Instead, she understood herself to be subordinated to her husband by the terms of scripture and her marriage contract. She was not to rule in the body but to be ruled by the word. Mary's rejection of her father in favor of loyalty to her husband affirmed the strength of contractual against dynastic ties. In the Glorious Revolution, as in the politics of the liberal family, the primacy of contract is predicated on the submission of women.

Three centuries later, the acceptance of the Declaration would be reenacted by a set of mechanized dolls installed in Whitehall, "the latest in presentation technology." The installation did, as promised, "vividly evoke" the effects of "the events of 1688–1689" on contemporary politics, though not quite with the promised facticity. The list of participants was much diminished (owing, no doubt, to the expense of reproducing so many legislators) and so was Mary's stature. Mary had been taller than her husband in the flesh. The cyber Mary sat, a head smaller, by his side. Though the installation at Whitehall would not note her political diminution, it had faithfully inscribed it on her body.[33]

The histories of the Glorious Revolution chronicle (as they secure) the affirmation of the rule of law, the rejection of divine right carried in a mortal body. This is the advent of modernity, the liberal order Locke inaugurates. Locke's refutation of Filmer expresses in philosophic form the altered constitution of the family immanent in the allegiances of William and Mary, the altered constitution of the regime immanent in the Declaration of Right, the lineaments of the order he read in (or perhaps, wrote into) the Glorious Revolution. Edmund Burke would be the creature and the critic of that order.

# 8
## The Jews of Change Alley

 urke's *Reflections on the Revolution in France* presents itself as a work on a present revolution in a foreign country. Within the work, however, Burke offers an account of England's past, a commentary on the Glorious Revolution. In reading France, Burke is writing England: constructing a history and constituting an identity for his own polity. This enterprise entails the construction not only of the French other but of a complex of identities alternately hidden and revealed in a delicate economy of memory and forgetting.

The French figure as the feminine partisans of abstract and universal principles: innovative, rational, and violent. The British are masculine, bound to their peculiar local practices: peaceful adherents to ancient and irrational customs. Each nation is made in memory. Each constitution is coupled with a characteristic mode of historiography. French historiography is the work of Enlightenment principles: investigative and revelatory. This is the historiography of bourgeois revolution, allied to an economy of praise and blame. British historiography mirrors the work of custom. The proper British historian, conscious of history as constitution, reads the present as memory made manifest: the work of time, with each practice possessing a primordial lineage. Nothing is lost, all is remembered. The "small and temporary deviations" that belie these claims of continuity are forgotten.

Burke writes two other histories in the margins of this account. These histories speak not only to the constitution of national identities but to the constitution of a more profound form of political order. In reading the history of France, Burke furnishes an antisemitic, and seemingly gratuitous, construction of the Jews. The lexicon of antisemitism supplies him with a series of metaphors that link modern with ancient enmities. In writing the history of England, Burke is silent on the Dutch. The Glorious Revolution, the work of a Dutch prince and an invading army, appears as a codification of English tradition, "drawn up by great lawyers and wise statesmen."[1] In his silence on the Dutch and his loquacious antisemitism, Burke registers his opposition to the ascendancy of contract and scriptural order.

The *Reflections on the Revolution in France* champions the particular in its form as well as in its content. Burke presents his history as a private letter, in which an older man instructs a younger. His correspondent had imagined, Burke writes, "that I might possibly be reckoned among the approvers of certain proceedings in France, from the solemn public seal of sanction they have received from two clubs of gentlemen in London, called the Constitutional Society and the Revolution Society." Burke, assuring his correspondent that he has "the honour to belong to more clubs than one, in which the constitution of this kingdom, and the principles of the Revolution are held in high reverence," moves rapidly to dissociate himself from the societies in question, acknowledging that each bears a name in conformity with his principles: "I am not . . . and have never been a member of either of those societies."[2] The Revolution Society comes in for particular condemnation. This society, inaugurated to commemorate the Glorious Revolution of 1688, had "long had the custom of hearing a sermon in one of their churches, and afterwards they spent the day cheerfully, as other clubs do, at the tavern." They had departed from this custom to issue and publicize a formal statement of support for the revolution in France. Burke, with no small sarcasm, writes, "Henceforward we must consider them as a kind of privileged persons; as no inconsiderable members in the diplomatic body." The Revolution Society's departure from accordance with custom to arrogation of privilege, from private to public activity, from the memory of an English Revolution to the acclamation of a French one, presents a multifaceted object for Burke's condemnation. The words with which he condemns them condemn the Jews.

Burke's letter disavows a set of resolutions and a sermon delivered by Dr. Richard Price "at the dissenting meeting-house of the Old Jewry."[3] Burke, who was wont to read meaning into place, refers to the partisans of the Revolution in England as "the Old Jewry" and writes thereafter of "the spurious revolutionary principles of the Old Jewry." Republican divines speak from the "Babylonian pulpits" of their English captivity, democrats commit apostasy and betray the kingdom for "thirty pieces of silver," and "Jews and jobbers" rely on usury and extortion.[4]

Why the Jews? The metaphoric logic of antisemitism, like Weberian analysis, associates scripture with law and lawyers, clerks, money, calculation, and the bureaucratic apparatus. For Burke, as for later and less learned antisemites, suspicion of the order of writing—of contractarianism—found metaphoric expression in the figure of the Jew. The Jews are the People of the Book. They are the chosen people of scripture. They bind texts upon their houses and their bodies. They write the law upon their inmost parts; they inscribe the covenant upon their bodies. They are bookish people, reading and writing, advancing in commerce, keeping accounts of history and trade, skilled in commercial and philosophic speculation. In them, writing is seen to overcome place, time, and the body.

The defenders of the French Revolution are "literary caballers and intriguing philosophers," phrases that call up the Kabballa.[5] Among them was George Gordon, Lord Byron, in Burke's words "a public proselyte to Judaism." In this case at least, the successors to the Israelites were to be found among the literati and in the camps of democratic revolution.

> We have let Lord George Gordon fast in Newgate. . . . Let him there meditate upon his Thalmud, until he learns a conduct more becoming to his birth and parts, and not so disgraceful to the ancient religion to which he has become a proselyte; or until some persons from your side of the water, to please your new Hebrew brethren, shall ransom him. He may then be enabled to purchase, with the old hoards of the synagogue, and a very small poundage, on the long compound interest of the thirty pieces of silver (Dr. Price has shown what miracles compound interest will perform in 1790 years) the lands which are lately discovered to have been usurped by the Gallican Church.[6]

Burke was not alone in identifying Judaism with Revolution. For Carlyle, it was the Americans who were the Jews, and he praised them for it. "Observe, however, beyond the Atlantic, has not the new day verily dawned? Democracy, as we said, is born; storm-girt, is struggling for life and victory. A sympathetic France rejoices over the Rights of Man; in all saloons it is said, What a spectacle! Now too behold our Deane, our Franklin, American Plenipotentiaries, here in person soliciting; the sons of the Saxon Puritans with their Old-Saxon Temper, Old-Hebrew Culture." Carlyle's revolutionary vignette is not without a certain antisemitism, it is "sleek Silas, sleek Benjamin" who are "soliciting." Yet even on such an errand, they stand in contrast to "the light children of Heathenism, Monarchy, Sentimentalism, and the Scarlet-woman." They appear in the form of Carlyle's much lauded Puritans, and in that form, as "Saxon-Puritans with their Old-Saxon temper, Old-Hebrew culture" make Hebrews of their Puritan ancestors.[7]

Carlyle and Burke concur in using the Jew as a metaphor for the partisans of scripture. Carlyle's Hebrew Puritans were part of the Good Old Cause, the Army of Scripture. Burke's French Revolutionaries and their fellow travelers in England adhered to more secular scriptures. The French, Burke charges, submit to the rule of lawyers and philosophes. "Property is destroyed" and they find themselves with "a paper circulation and a stock-jobbing constitution."[8] The English partisans of the revolution menace the country with the ascendancy of men of letters, abstract philosophy and a calculative rationality. Burke asks, "Is every landmark of the country to be done away with in favor of a geometrical and arithmetical constitution? . . . Are the Church lands to be sold to Jews and jobbers?"[9]

The future that menaces England is already present in France. Burke challenges the French revolutionaries, "Compute your gains: see what is got by those extravagant and presumptuous speculations." "France has bought undisguised calamity at a higher price than any nation has purchased the most unequivocal blessings! France has bought poverty by crime!"[10]

Burke's antisemitism is profound. The Jews are identified not only with money but with a moral economy. In recognizing the link between the money economy and the moral economy of guilt, recompense, revenge, and retribution, Burke anticipates Nietzsche. The Jews are not mere usurers in Burke's analysis. They are those who keep a moral and historical accounting.

The project of estimation and assessment, of the determination of worth, is transformed (as Nietzsche recognized) from a monetary to a moral economy, from *schulden* to *schuld*.[11] The accounting Burke condemned—the accounting Burke feared—was not economic but ethical. The old order had been weighed in the balance and found wanting. Now those who had profited from those arrangements—the monarchy, the nobility, the church—would be called to account. "All the decent drapery of life is to be torn off. All the superadded ideas, furnished from the wardrobe of a moral imagination . . . to cover the defects of our naked, shivering nature and to raise it to dignity in our own estimation, are to be exploded."[12] Burke knew well what any scrutiny would reveal: "naked, shivering nature," bodies like any other bodies, though perhaps better fed, stripped of their concealments and exposed with all the marks of their humanity—and their excesses—upon them. He saw as clearly as the sans-culottes that "On this scheme of things, a king is but a man, a queen is but a woman, a woman is but an animal; and an animal not of the highest order."[13] Burke might have been more apt if he were more colloquial: on this scheme, the queen was but a woman, and a woman no better than she should be. Burke's French revolutionaries, like Nietzsche's Egyptian youth, were seized by an unseemly passion to reveal the truth, "in all the nakedness and solitude of metaphysical abstraction."[14]

Revolutionary historians, and the philosophes who directed them, would make a strict accounting. They would check the books of their predecessors, examine their titles, assess their duties and their fulfillment of those duties, determine responsibility, and hold all to account. These historians were investigators, prosecuters, judges; calculators of praise and blame. They were allied with the project of revolutionary enlightenment.

Burke recognized the intimate relation between sight and judgment in an early letter on the revolution: "what Spectators, and what actors! England gazing with astonishment at a French struggle for liberty and not knowing whether to blame or to applaud!"[15] The passion for enlightenment that swept through the salons and the Tuileries, that tore open the Bastille and the body of the king, that called for an end to secrecy and a beginning to surveillance, was accompanied by a passionate call for justice.

The exposure of the ancien regime was a festival of enlightenment and equality, stripping away the old concealments, the old illusions, the old trappings of pretentious authority. Burke protests against this understanding of history as discovery. Against a history allied to the call for an accounting, Burke looks for a history "better understood, and better employed," a didactic history, a history that will "teach."[16] For Burke, history is the search for a usable past, a past that will furnish materials for the construction of a constitution. He tells the French: "Your constitution, it is true, while you were out of possession, suffered waste, and dilapidation; but you possessed in some parts the walls, and, in all, the foundations, of a noble and venerable castle. You might have repaired those walls, you might have built on those old foundations."[17] Constitution, for Burke, is not the invention of a moment, but the work of years in which each generation builds upon the work—and the ruins— of the past. History, for Burke, is not the activity of discovery but the art of exegesis, in which each generation reads its presence in—or into— the past.

This is the history Burke writes for Britain. In Burke's exemplary British history, "the succession of the crown has always been what it now is: succession by law: in the old line it was a succession by the common law, in the new by the statute law."[18] One might see considerable changes in that lineage of sameness. Theological disturbances are as carefully cloaked: "Four hundred years have gone over us; but I believe we are not materially changed since that period." "So tenacious are we of the old ecclesiastical modes and fashions of institution, that very little alteration has been made in them since the fourteenth or fifteenth century."[19]

Burke's forgetfulness of civil war, his easy glossing over of the transmutation of common law to statute law, of the authority of the body of the ruler to the authority of the rule, are not, however, the sophistries they seem. Nor are Burke's historical fictions mere mystifications. For Burke, the "natural" was that which accorded with the nature in question, that which was consistent with the ordering of the whole, that which conformed to the order present in its constitution. History was the act of reading a constitutional order in disorder; the exegesis of a cryptic past. Burke's history is in the service of the British constitution. In his reading endurance, tenacity, and an inherited estate become the peculiar qualities of the British. "From Magna Charta to the Declaration of Right, it has been the uniform policy of our constitution to claim and assert our liberties, as an *entailed inheritance* derived to us from our forefathers, and to be transmitted to our posterity; as an estate especially belonging to the people of this kingdom."[20] With a few well-chosen words, Burke makes moments of revolutionary change into the horizon of continuity, the temporal boundary-markers of a nation. In remembering the limits and definitions that emerged from these events, Burke would have his readers forget the conflicts, ambiguities, absences, and openings that produced them. From moments when the nation was open to question, Burke fashions the closure of the body politic.

The Glorious Revolution is not, for Burke, the triumph of writing over flesh and blood, but writing used to clothe naked shivering nature, to provide the concealments that will lend the English dignity in their own estimation. The naked power of William's invading army is clothed in letters and documents. The English are to forget that the Glorious Revolution was the work of a Dutch invader. They are to remember that William was "a prince of the blood royal."

Burke is no defender of the divine right. He is for a "manly, moral, regulated, liberty."[21] Mary, therefore, whose title is in the blood, must take second place to William, whose title comes through blood and the law. Burke knows that Mary had the stronger claim to the throne, both by right of birth and by the favor of Parliament. "There is no person so completely ignorant of our history as not to know, that the majority in Parliament . . . were determined to place the vacant Crown, not on the head of the Prince of Orange, but on that of his wife Mary, daughter of King James."[22] This is very deft. In a single sentence Burke disposes of both the claim that Parliament determines the succession and the claims of blood alone. If Parliament declined, at that most favorable time, to establish the principle that "a king of popular choice was the only legal king," they affirmed "that the nation was of the opinion that it ought not to be done at any time."[23] Those who did not wish to "to recall King James or to deluge their country in blood" were obliged to prefer William. For Burke, "accepting King William was not properly a choice . . . it was an act of *necessity,* in the strictest moral sense in which necessity can be taken."[24] They were not compelled to the choice by adherence to an inalterable principle, for, as Burke noted, "unquestionably, there was at the Revolution, in the person of King William, a small and a temporary deviation from the strict order of a regular hereditary succession." Nor were they compelled by force. They were compelled by the demands of time, the press of circumstances. They were compelled by the demands of history and prudence.

Burke writes very carefully. William is "the Prince of Orange," later, "King William." Mary is given no title and is referred to through her relations with men; "his wife, Mary, daughter of King James." William is elevated not by blood alone (though he is "a prince of the blood royal") nor by Parliamentary acts alone, but by "a small and temporary deviation" from a strict order. Neither the rule of the blood, nor the rule of writing will find a vindication in Burke. The Revolution is made Glorious by this "small and temporary deviation."[25] In it the demands of time and temporality triumph over abstraction. The statesmen of the Revolution attended to the conditions of a particular time and country, the talents of particular men. Their glory lies in their prudence.

The effacement of Mary, of feminine power, is central to Burke's project. He seeks the establishment of a "manly, moral, and regulated liberty."[26] He is the partisan of "severer manners, and a system of a more austere and masculine morality."[27] The French Republic, in Burke's account, has the head of Medusa. The Revolution takes on the form of "the furies of hell, in the abused shape of the vilest of women."[28]

> France, when she let loose the reins of regal authority, doubled the licence of ferocious dissoluteness in manners, and of an insolent irreligion in opinions and practices; and has extended through all ranks of life, as if she were communicating some privilege, or laying open some secluded benefit, all the unhappy corruptions that were usually the disease of wealth and power. This is one of the new principles of equality in France.[29]

Burke associates openness with the loss of moral—and bodily—integrity. The open body politic is dissolute, lacking the restraints of prudence or religion. "France has abandoned her interest, that she might prostitute her virtue." The open body is feminine. The open body is the body corrupted. The open body politic is ferocious, and ungovernable.

The English have preserved their integrity:

> In England we have not been completely embowelled of our natural entrails; we still have within us, and we cherish and cultivate, those inbred sentiments which are . . . the true supporters of all liberal and manly morals.[30]

The closed body preserves its morals with its entrails. The closed body is the masculine, moral, liberal body. Burke differs from other liberal thinkers, however, in associating writing not with the closing but with the opening of the body.

> We have not been drawn and trussed, in order that we may be filled, like stuffed birds in a museum, with chaff and rags and paltry blurred shreds of paper about the rights of man.[31]

The closed body preserves, in Burke, "inbred sentiments," prejudices written in the blood. Men of "untaught feelings" prefer their prejudices to their reason, knowing that the "private stock of reason" is small against "the general bank and capital of nations and of ages." Consideration of time, in Burke, leads one to prefer prejudice to rationality.

> Prejudice is of ready application in the emergency; it previously engages the mind in a steady course of wisdom and virtue, and does not leave the man hesitating in the moment of decision; skeptical, puzzled and unresolved.[32]

Not reason, but prejudice gives closure in Burke's view. "Prejudice renders a man's virtue his habit; and not a series of unconnected acts. Through just prejudice, his duty becomes part of his nature."[33] In this habitual virtue acts are bound together; the man made thus made whole submits, without thought, to duty.[34] Prejudice binds him to his place, his time, his land, his people. Prejudice gives closure. Thought, Burke recognized, is the activity of solitude, the province of the aporia.

Constituted by just prejudices,

> we preserve the whole of our feelings native and entire. . . . We fear God; we look up with awe to kings; with affection to Parliament; with duty to magistrates; with reverence to priests; and with respect to nobility. Why? Because when such ideas are brought before our minds it is *natural* to be so affected.[35]

This nature is not man as he comes from the hand of the Author of things, nor man as he comes from the womb of a woman. This is the nature of a man born to a community and a place in it, to a time and a time past, to a people and a history not of his own making.

The Glorious Revolution that Burke writes is a peculiarly English event, the work of time in a particular place, conceived not in the crisis of a moment, nor in response to external influences, but in the uninterrupted evolution of one people's common law. The peculiar terms of the settlement emerge from English circumstances and English inclinations. The genealogy that secures the Revolution within the law is a wholly English genealogy. The inclination to endurance, to continuity, to the "slight deviation" and particular solution, are characteristics of English policy. Burke's history, like all histories, depends on an economy of memory and forgetting. England must remember the English ancestry, the English circumstances, the English qualities of the Glorious Revolution. England must forget that it is indebted to the Dutch.

# 9
## Dutch William

The Dutch polity was the open body politic. The Netherlands lacked all forms of definition. Held together in a constantly negotiated arrangement, the States, the Republic, the United Provinces had neither a settled name nor settled political arrangements.[1] The citizens, subjects, refugees, and other inhabitants shared neither religion nor language nor ethnicity. They were not bounded even by the sea. The Dutch were inhabitants of "the universal quagmire," "such an equilibrium of earth and water that a strong earthquake would shake them into a chaos."[2] Their borders were constantly uncertain: changed by war and nature certainly, but also by their own labor.

> They, with mad labor, fished the land to shore,
> And dived as desperately for each piece
> Of earth as if't had been of ambergris . . .
> Who best could learn to pump an earth so leak
> Him they their Lord, and Country's Father, speak
> To make a bank was a great plot of state;
> Invent a shovel and be a magistrate.[3]

In the Netherlands of Marvell's imagining, social boundaries are as fragile and permeable as a Dutch dike. Rank is secured by labor: labor of the most manual and prosaic. This was a nation (or if not a nation, a people) of Diggers. The Dutch in Marvell's poem revive an older, English, question:

> When Adam delved and Eve span
> Who was then the gentleman?

Yet these Diggers and delvers, fishermen and traders, were adept at conquest. They took land from the sea. On occasion they even took it from the French. They extended their colonial possessions. They ventured out beyond their boundaries and came home in ships laden with luxuries unknown to an envious aristocracy. One could not be certain, therefore, if the uncertainty of Dutch boundaries was a sign of their fragility or of their power.

Condemnations of the "dunghill soul" of the Dutch referred to their extraordinary productive capacities, their great wealth, and (through a commonplace inversion) their preoccupation with cleanliness. The Dutch are, however, not merely envied for their wealth; they are feared for their transformative power. In Gillray's *Opening the Sluices,* Dutch women (and a helpful frog) open their bodies and drown their enemies. In another satiric print, the Dutch women's productive capacities are aided by men who pour gin into them. These satiric prints conflate the open body with the power of production and circulation: the transformative power of Dutch capitalism.[4]

The Dutch unsettled not only their nation but their neighbors'. They were "the greatest patrons of Schism in the world." Their presses printed philosophy, religion, and sedition for the whole of Europe.

> Hence Amsterdam, Turk-Christian-Pagan-Jew
> Staple of sects and mint of schism grew;
> That bank of conscience, where not one so strange
> Opinion, but finds credit and exchange.[5]

Thoughts circulated like money and, like money, multiplied in speculation. Burke castigated the Jacobins, whose object, as he saw it, was to turn France

> into one great play-table; to turn its inhabitants into a nation of gamesters; to make speculation as extensive as life; to mix it with all its concerns.[6]

For many of Burke's countrymen, images of calculation, abstract speculation, seditious reasoning and hard accounting, republicanism, change, disorder, and a political body in flux belonged not to the Jew or the Jacobin, but to the Dutch.

"They are the Israelites," Owen Felltham wrote. The Dutch knew themselves to be booksellers and moneylenders to Europe, traders and financiers. They were a people who had lived under captivity and been delivered from it, a people brought out of slavery, a people who had known the singular favor of providence. They knew they were not as the nations. They were a people of the covenant. For James Gillray it was not the Jacobins but the Dutch who "leave nothing unpolluted with the slime of their filthy offal."[7] The Dutch had long ago surpassed the French in speculation. It was in the Netherlands that fortunes were made and lost not on a tulip but on the possibility of a tulip.

The Netherlands were the provinces of the material imaginary: money and goods made imaginary, made to circulate, made to increase through speculation. The Netherlands were the provinces of the imaginary made material: tulips of imagined colors and forms, trading expeditions, and a design for Europe, were conceived, cultivated, and realized here.

This is the motherland of speculation, of the free circulation of words and thought, great enterprises and simple pleasures. This is the imaginary homeland of bourgeois virtue. These Dutch have well-furnished houses filled with exotic goods, with gardens and menageries, with well-fed and well-dressed people. This disorderly nation has clean people, clean houses, and clean streets. Always unsatisfied with their nation and themselves, always wanting more: more goods and more self-restraint, more profit and more charity, more liberties and more possessions. This is a nation of invention and innovation. This is the womb of bourgeois revolution. This is the future of Burke's fears.

This was the nation of Dutch William. Burke would have us see the Glorious Revolution as a event of English making, a long growth of law, and King William as a prince of the blood royal. But William was "Dutch William" to the English, with his Dutch friends, Dutch manners, and Dutch tastes. The English, then and since, saw in William the hazards of an open body politic.

Satiric poetry of the period made accusations of sodomy a constant theme in attacks on William. "William van Nassau with Benting Bardasha, / Are at the old game of Gomorrah"[8] "He is not qualified for his wife. . . . Yet buggering of Benting doth please to the life."[9] Other poems refer to Bentinck as William's "he-bedfellow" and claim that William "makes statesmen of blockheads and Earls of bardashes."

> . . . your love is Italian, your Government Dutch
> Ah! Who could have thought that a Low Country stallion
> And a Protestant Prince should prove an Italian?[10]

The charges persist into our own time. The author of a volume on William and Mary in a series of royal biographies aimed at a popular audience writes, "Much controversy has centred around William's relationships with men. The two courtiers most often singled out for rumours of the King's homosexuality were William Bentinck . . . and the younger Arnold Joost van Keppel." Even as it insists sedately "this cannot be proven or disproven, but it seems unlikely," the volume dwells on "Keppel's rather effeminate good looks" and the intensity of William's preference for male companionship.[11] Virtually every biographical work cites Gilbert Burnet's cryptic "He had no vice, but of one sort, in which he was very cautious and secret" and interprets it as a reference to homosexual practices. Jonathan Swift added, "It was of two sorts, male and female, and in the former he was neither cautious nor secret." One records rumors of "frequent private and lengthy visits to William's rooms of a handsome young captain of the cavalry" and speculates on the character of his relations with his friends, concluding somewhat disingenuously, "To what extent these relationships were homosexual is difficult to discover."[12]

In an earlier Stuart court satiric treatments of expansive sexuality carried an aura of transgressive play and illicit pleasure. They spoke, however critically, to the unbounded sexuality of the monarch and the aristocracy, reinforcing their claims to power in the flesh. William was by no means the first king, or the first Stuart, to be accused of illicit sexual practices. In William's case, however, these are associated not with the excesses but with the political failure of the flesh.

> And Billy with Benting doth play the Italian. . . .
> Midst such blessed pairs, succession prevails,
> And if Nan of Denmark or Dutch Molly fails,
> May pregnant Mynheer spawn a new Prince of Wales.[13]

This piece furnishes another oblique recognition of the erasure of the feminine, and the transition from the power of the flesh to the power of the word. Hume writes that "the advantage of the Hanover succession . . . arise from this very circumstance, that it violates hereditary right and places on the throne a prince, to whom birth gave no title to that dignity." Hume's dismissive reference to "such a specious title as that of blood" and his declaration that "an anatomist finds no more in the greatest monarch than in the lowest day-labourer; and a moralist may, perhaps, frequently find less" demonstrate how successful the

Revolution had been at securing the claims of the word of law over those of the flesh.[14]

Readings of William's sexuality—then and now—show the limits of this turn from the flesh to the word. In an interview on the discourse of homosexuality, Michel Foucault declared, "The development toward which the problem of homosexuality tends is the one of friend-ship." Images of homosexual sex, however transgressive, are reassur-ing, Foucault observes, because they annul

> everything that can be uncomfortable in affection, tenderness, friend-ship, fidelity, camaraderie, companionship, things which our rather sanitized society can't allow a place for without fearing the formation of new alliances and the tying together of unforeseen lines of force.

"To imagine a sexual act that doesn't conform to law or nature is not what disturbs people," Foucault argues.[15]

Contemporary accounts of his practices and character, and his long correspondence with William Bentinck, leave William's sexual preferences and practices in question. They leave no doubt, however, that William's friendship with Bentinck was passionate and familiar, or that Bentinck held first place in William's loves and loyalties. The force of William's preference for friendship over kinship marked the court not only in the bestowing of titles and other benefits but in the demarcation of public and private space. For William, not only public but private space and status were to be constituted by the word rather than the flesh.

We are still bound, we of this long age, in an order constituted in the constant transubstantiations of the word and flesh. The triumph of the word of the law over the power of the flesh did not displace the latter. The confessional imperative, casting flesh into words, "was a way of placing sexuality at the heart of existence."[16] There it remains. In our time, as in William's, friendship is "a manner of being that is still improbable."[17]

The Dutch education that William would bring to England and America did, however, establish the foundations for allegiances rooted in affinity rather than sexuality. Covenant and contract, the obliga-tions of national allegiance and the proprieties of church and market had made the Dutch modern subjects: people of the text.

The Dutch saw themselves as children of the covenant. They looked, as another republic had done, to be ruled by the word. William was a passionate Dutchman, a nationalist leader who had heard himself hailed as Hezekiah.[18] He was Prince of Orange, but in the iconography of his youth the princes of Orange knelt with the States before the liberty cap, under the tetragrammaton, the letters of the name of God.[19] William, a prince brought to power by Parliament, and Cromwell, an autocrat brought to power by republicans, both presented, in iconic form, the constitutive contradiction of the British mixed constitution, the government that lapsed republicans had named "parliament and a single person." This, their status as the champions of Protestantism, their martial character, and the republics that stood behind and before them, made images of Oliver Cromwell and William interchangeable. Satiric poetry employed the same trope. One set of verses is entitled "On the Late Metamorphosis of an Old Picture of Oliver Cromwell into a New Picture of King William: The Head Changed, the Hieroglyphics Remaining." As the spectators debate the identification of the portrait of William, one speaks up authoritatively.

> 'Tis good King William. See Rome trampled down.
> See his triumphant foot on papists' necks.
> See Salus Populi Suprema Lex.
> See Magna Charta. Can all this agree
> With any man but Oliver and he?[20]

William's accession collapsed the Cromwellian and Carolinean successions. Cromwell was succeeded by the son of his body, and then by the restoration of the king. The second Charles Stuart returned to England by invitation, preceded by a declaration.[21] Cromwell came to power through bloodshed: regicide and the bloody triumphs of the army. The second Charles Stuart claimed his title through inheritance and had unsuccessfully attempted to come to the throne through war. The intervention of generals and parliamentarians was necessary to secure his accession. Later historians would see his restoration as the work of another Dutch education. Charles Stuart owed the return of monarchy to the work of General Monk. "Monk had first served in the Dutch armies, where, as he put it, soldiers received and obeyed orders. His whole career can be interpreted as displaying a respect for civil authority."[22] Throughout his reign Charles Stuart endeavored (with more shrewdness and subtlety than his brother) to distance himself from dependence on Parliament and to make possible the continuance of rule by right of blood. William came to the throne through writing: Protestant scripture, a letter of invitation, the Declaration of

Right, a marriage contract, and a contract with Parliament. In his rule as well as his accession, the power of blood (bloodshed as well as blood ties) was subordinated to the rule of law and the authority of Parliament.

William brought to England his Dutch sense of politics: a respect for republican legislatures and the capacity to work within a changing, often disordered polity. The Declaration of Rights echoed the language of William's earlier Declaration; it was shaped by his direction and concerns. William's access to information from the convention and to figures within it, his understanding of the degree of influence he might bring to bear and the avenues he could appropriately employ, and the discretion that marked his conduct were the consequences of a long education in republican politics.[23] In his dealings with Parliament William appears as the executive in a legal rational order: empowered by the methods and constrained by the limits he had learned as stadholder. William brought to the monarchy an educated sense of accountability in office. He taught the British the duties of a constitutional monarch. The order he inaugurated in his example was the issue of a Dutch education. The Dutch order that William brought to England held the threat of Dutch disorder—the menace, or the promise of an order yet to come—within it.

The unsettled structures of the Dutch republic are instructive. They apprised Spinoza, and through Spinoza, Antonio Negri, of the order present in the multitude. "This right exists not because of the force of the greater number of people, but because of the constitution of the greater number. The greater number of people, starting precisely from the natural enmity that forms their behaviour, begin to constitute a political and a juridical body."[24] Contending desires prompt the conception of abstract standards of need and right. Differences in ends necessitate negotiation, and the conception of common objects. Without conflict, commonalty will remain unconscious, unconceived.

Immanent in the unsettled structures of the Dutch republic is an order in which the one and the many, order and disorder, aporia and definition are no longer opposed. Here the definition of nationality reveals itself as the consequence not of closure but of a contentious, aporetic identity. Here unity is the work of many, in contention rather than consensus. Here the one is one only because it remains manifold.

The Dutch make visible the open body of bourgeois revolution. Theirs is not only the daring rapacity of a commercial and consumerist capitalism. Theirs is a body politic open to empire and to innovation, to philosophic and financial speculation, to the entrance of the alien and the abandonment of tradition. These are a people open to changes in their customs and their borders, to changes in themselves. This is a revolutionary nation with the appetites of the aristocracy, a people impelled by the inappeasable desire for more.

# Section 3

# 10
## Revolutionary Memories

What is remembered of revolutions? Americans remember words. They celebrate their revolution on the Fourth of July and date their independence from 1776. On that day the Declaration of Independence was read before the people and acquired authority in their acclamation. Americans remember their founding as an act of revolution. They remember that revolution as an act of speech and writing, a genesis in words.

In France, it was the fall of the Bastille that made a memory for the nation. July 14, the anniversary of that day, recalls the revolution. In the memory of the French the beginnings of the republic are "like the beginnings of all things great on earth, soaked in blood thoroughly, and for a very long time."[1]

We remember the revolutions in France and America as acts of writing and violence. It was through writing and through violence, in ink and blood, that these revolutions inscribed themselves on the world, writing their law upon the inmost parts of their people. They are remembered through writing and violence. They are as they are remembered, for the creation of memory is not the mark but the making of nations, of revolutions, of peoples.

The French and American revolutions, and the peoples they made, were constituted between the poles of writing and violence. In America, the revolution is said to have begun, with the nation, in the Declaration of Independence. The nation was spoken into being. This engendering word, the annunciation of the nation, is followed by the violence of revolution. In the midst of the Revolutionary War, words and violence follow fast on one another. They are bound together in Patrick Henry's demand "Give me liberty or give me death" and in Paul Revere's warning "The British are coming!" We recall the fall of Fort Ticonderoga in the words Ethan Allen used to arrest the British commander: "in the name of the Great God Jehovah and the Continental Congress." Words establish the nation in the American conception, violence defends it, and words secure the victory.

The violence of the revolution would be succeeded by another act of founding, the words of the Constitution. Not only the nation but its government would be born in words. In these words Americans attempted to secure a collective memory for themselves and their posterity. Generations have returned to those words in the recollection, ritual and quotidian, of their nationality.

In France it is the fall of the Bastille that is celebrated as the beginning of the revolution. It was preceded by an outpouring of words. The collective memory of the French, whether in academic or popular history, directs our gaze to the lettres de cachet. The letters, we read, made the Bastille a hated object. Knowledge of these hidden letters, these unread words, was behind the attack. In the provinces, as in Paris, writings prefigured acts of violence. Before the revolution, before the uprisings of the peasant and the bourgeois and the sans-culottes, there were the *cahiers de doléances.* In the cahiers, old grievances, often spoken, more often suppressed, were cast into a new and revolutionary form. An American might date the French Revolution from the cahiers or the Tennis Court Oath. In France not the words but the violence of revolution founds the republic. It begins on July 14, 1789.

Saint Just, in a speech before the convention, dated the revolution differently: "The Revolution begins when the tyrant ends."[2] For him it was another act of violence, the execution of Louis Capet, that marked the revolution's triumph and begat the nation. Behind this act, in the hopes and fears, the tactics and the affectations, the institutions and the ceremonials of the revolution, one reads the words of the philosophes. In France, and more profoundly outside it, the French Revolution is remembered for the violence of the Terror. In that great outpouring of blood not only the history of the French Revolution but the course of many revolutions to come were written.

The revolutions in America and France alternately conceal and reveal themselves in the iridescent relation of writing and violence. They are alike in the presence and rapidity of transubstantiation: from blood to words, from words to blood. Both peoples seal their promises in words and blood. Memory (if not practice) grants primacy to writing in America, to violence in France, and writing and violence take different forms in each.

The French and American revolutions, both marked by writing, show writing in two different forms. In America, writing is a form of revelation. Whether one looks to the Declaration of Independence or to the Constitution for the founding, one finds writing used to make authority public, to make the people visible. The Declaration displays the people to the world, begetting a nation through annunciation. It demands publicity, presenting its catalogue of injustices to a candid world. The Declaration unmasks the malfeasance of George and his ministers, and in doing so it ends his rule. It declares the Americans independent, displaying them, for the first time, as a nation to a watching world. Like another scripture, these writings base their authority on revelation. They reveal a comprehensive being, begotten in speech. They reveal certain fundamental truths, prior to speech and reason: "We hold these truths to be self-evident, that all men are created equal, that they are endowed by their Creator with certain inalienable rights, that among these are Life, Liberty, and the Pursuit of Happiness." These rights, not dependent on recognition or consent, are presented as a revelation.

The Declaration is remembered in writing. One can still find inscriptions—in a corridor at the University of Pennsylvania, in small towns in Virginia, Delaware, and Massachusetts—marking places where the Declaration was first read before the people. Of all those who signed the Declaration, Americans remember John Hancock best, writing his name more boldly than the rest, calling on the king to read it. The people display their authority with equal boldness, and in the same fashion, in the Constitution, writing their name in a larger, bolder script, inscribing their authority, in writing, on their Constitution. In this gesture Americans mark not only their own authority but the authority of writing. It is in writing that they assert their authority and, through writing, the simple act of making some words larger than the rest, that they inscribe on the text itself a recognition of writing as authoritative.

In America, public writings found regimes. In France, secret writings, once discovered, bring them down. Writing serves, in the French Revolution, not only as a form of display but as a disguise. In the constitutive events and documents of that revolution one can read a commentary on writing as form of rule. Writing that records, that classifies, that reports, is marked as a means to power, an attribute of authority. Such writing sees the ruled but need not be seen by them.

This is the writing of the lettres de cachet. Two things are hidden in these letters; the prisoner who will be put away, and the true author of the letter, which comes in the name of the king. Those who struck at the lettres de cachet, and at the fortress that had become the sign of their power, struck at these veiled authors.

In the country, the peasants labored under the burden of rights conferred, it was claimed, in writing on their lords and landlords. The peasant rebels of earlier centuries had seized and burned the records of châteaux, hoping to erase oppression with the title to it. As resistance surfaced again in the eighteenth century, peasants undertook lawsuits to uncover the documents and dispute their claims. Those who demanded that lords and proprietors produce the documents and name the authors that conferred seigneurial rights saw this unmasking of the author as a blow to authority.

The remembered revolution in France shows writing not as a form of revelation but as an instrument of rule. In American memory, the author is invested with power by acts of self-annunciation. In France, writing confers the capacity to conceal oneself, and power follows from this. The author is veiled, and power is exercised by a hidden hand.

This understanding of power was not confined to the ancien regime. Those who employed anonymous petitions to denounce their enemies to the Committee on Public Safety, who kept (as such committees tend to keep) secret records of dissidents and suspects, who hid their authority as they exercised it, also wrote to rule. They marked this disguise, the absence of a name, as an attribute of—and a means to—authority.

The adoption of the practice of surveillance as an instrument and the "œil de surveillance" as a sign of authority speak of an author as one who sees but remains himself unseen. The Bastille calls up Bentham and Foucault, two who saw the power of sight to rule. Bentham, Foucault writes, "laid down the principle that power should be visible and unverifiable."[3] As the prisoners in the Panopticon saw the tower from which they were observed but not the watching authority, who remained concealed, so the governed should see the holders of authority but not what lay within them.

This principle may have been first laid down by Bentham, but it had been put in practice long before. The eminently visible Bastille had a concealed and mysterious interior. The palaces of the King, conspicuous without, concealed all within. The body of the king, seen in the spectacles of the court, on coins, in statues and portraits, caricatures and effigies, contained an invisible authority, an illegible title. The fortress, the palaces, the body of the king, and the dress and manners of the aristocrats all made power visible and concealed authority. Authority belonged, in France as elsewhere, to those who could make their power visible and remain concealed.

This economy of secrecy and display called forth what Foucault called "the Rousseauist dream," "the dream of a transparent society, visible and legible in each of its parts, the dream of there no longer existing any zones of darkness, zones established by the privileges of royal power . . . the dream that each individual, whatever position he occupied, might be able to see the whole of society."[4] This dream took foreign form in America. There the Rousseauist dream became not flesh but word. The canonical—the constitutional—American documents display the desire of the people, of the regime, to display itself, to be at once reader and author, to see and be seen. When writing serves as revelation, ruler and ruled are made equal. In the Declaration, the authors call upon the world to approve their authority, making themselves not only the holders of authority but its subjects. The people make themselves author and text in their constitution; they write and make themselves subject to writing. Casting the preamble in the present tense, they call upon later generations, on all others, to join them in their authority. Equality, and the reciprocity of rule, are written into the regime.

Writing had the ascendancy in America, but both the passion for bloodshed and the passion for inscription were stronger in France than in America. There were proposals in the Jacobin clubs and in more moderate circles for citizens to inscribe on every lintel "Liberty, Equality, Fraternity" and other revolutionary sentiments. Monuments were erected, banners carried, rooms painted with the tricolor. Within these rooms, there were statues of Reason, Liberty, and Marianne, busts of Marat and Lepeletier.

Citizens were obliged, by their own patriotic sentiments or those of their neighbors, to wear the tricolor. The king was obliged, by demanding sans-culottes, to wear a Liberty cap. People marked their revolutionary sentiments on their clothing, wearing a sort of revolutionary deshabille or (writing on their clothes what they read in their books) fashions that recalled those of earlier republics.

Before the high writing of the Declaration of the Rights of Man and of the Citizen, there had been the cahiers; before the constitutions, the writings of the philosophes. After them, there were new laws, a new flag, and a new currency. There were new records of births and deaths and marriages, and new sorts of records. Citizens of the republic, if they were fortunate and deserving, could obtain *certificats de civisme*, providing them with (written) revolutionary credentials.

The land, like the lives, of the French was rewritten in the records and altered in appearance. The country was newly divided into departments. The landscape was inscribed with artificial Mountains and trees of Liberty. Time itself was altered. The revolution gave a new history to the people of France, and it did more. The division of the land into new departments was paralleled by the division of the days and seasons in the revolutionary calendar. The revolution wrote its regard for rationality into the decade, it wrote its regard for nature in the names of the months. The calendar was inscribed with the memories of the revolution. Year I began with the demise of feudalism.

The inscription of the revolution on the land, on time, in private homes and public records, was only the outward sign, the mark, of the inscription of the law on the people. The citizens of France sang new songs; "La Marseillaise" and, for a while, "Ça Ira." They were taught new prayers, new litanies, new professions of faith, and new acts of contrition. They were given new festivals, new rituals, new saints, and new catechisms.[5]

There were monuments in America, Liberty trees, and pictures of George Washington; there were new laws, a new flag, and a new currency. There was not this passion for inscription, writing its rule on the world. There was not the conscious effort of the revolution to "write its law upon their inmost parts." The catechisms of the Jacobins lack an American counterpart, as do those acts that literally inscribed the law of the revolution on the entrails of its victims. In America, enemies of the nation and the revolution were shot, bayoneted, stabbed, and occasionally hung, almost always on the battlefield. Then they were buried. In France they were shot, bayoneted, stabbed, and hung on the battlefields and in the streets. They were guillotined. They were burned. If they were killed by the mob, they might have their hands cut off before their deaths, or their heads cut off after. Severed heads might be paraded on pikes. Hearts were cut out, blood was drunk, entrails eaten (raw or cooked) or at least tasted. Not only the quantity but the quality of violence differed in France and America.

In France, writing took on the character of transubstantiation. Acts of violence became words; a date in the calendar a description of an event, or partisans. One still speaks of Thermidor and the *septembriseurs*. Often acts of violence, occasioned by some ill-chosen words, were themselves written like texts. Foullon de Doue, a minister in the government of Breteuil, was said to have remarked that the people should eat hay if they were hungry. He had his mouth stuffed with hay before his head was cut off.[6] The abolition of the monarchy was made material in the death of the king. Louis himself referred, on the scaffold, to "les auteurs de ma mort." To this day, it is remembered of those who ruled in the Terror that their words became their end. They wrote the laws and the dictates, they founded the committees, they wrote and read the lists and signed the papers that sent people to the guillotine, and in the end they came to it themselves. They were defined, given their meaning and their ends, by the Terror they authored.

This is not to say, as many have said before, that the American Revolution was a pallid prefiguration of that robustly sanguine enterprise in France. The revolution in America brought down the Church and the aristocracy more surely than the revolution in France. Though they would hesitate and backslide, permitting, in the nineteenth century, more intimacy between state and clergy than the deistical Founders would have tolerated, they would maintain the sovereignty of the secular. Though they would see the rise of robber barons and Boston Brahmins, though they would begin to detach titles from offices and attach them, undemocratically, to persons, they would never again acknowledge aristocratic claims.

It has become commonplace to claim that the French undertook a more thorough revolution because they had more to pull down. Perhaps. America lacked a formal religious establishment, a single Church, but it possessed religious enthusiasts who would astonish Tocqueville. Americans, particularly Americans in New England, had been ruled by their clerics. They retained their faith, for the most part, and with it gave sanction and legitimacy to an authority that might have challenged the secular, irreverent revolution. Yet the revolution, and the state it established, maintained their sovereignty. America had those who boasted titles and those who lusted after them, state after state where men prided themselves on their birth and could recite the genealogies of their neighbors and their horses to the tenth generation. Americans held slaves. Yet these held, more surely than the descendants of the soi-disant Égalité, to the declaration that all men are created equal. The Americans who once addressed the king would set him aside whole, yet they would never restore the monarchy. It was the recognition of the somewhat more thorough success of the revolution in America that prompted Paine to call for the exile of the French king to America.

The objects of French revolutionary violence, animate and inanimate, testify to the fears and enmities of the revolution. Revolutionaries on the march and in the streets stormed the Bastille and the Tuileries. Orders issued from one, people entered the other and were seen no more, but in each case the interior was a place of power and secrecy, which the people were not permitted to enter or behold. The attacks opened these places to the sight of the people. After the Bastille fell and before it was razed, it was made a public exhibit, and crowds of Parisians wandered through the fortress. The market women who invaded Versailles sat on the chairs and the beds and the furniture as if to claim them. They looked into the drawers and closets and explored the rooms. Peasants in the countryside demanded that their lords make public the documents that conferred seigneurial rights. They attacked places where grain was said to be hoarded. They too opened formerly hidden places of authority to the public gaze. Privacy, the capacity to conceal oneself from the gaze of the people, was a sign, perhaps a form, of power. It was undone in the opening of these secret places.

The acts of revolutionaries were acts of revelation. They opened secret places, they made hidden machinations visible. The sansculottes opened the Bastille and the Tuileries, the philosophes looked into other matters. The inquiries, the investigations, the speculations, and the theories of the Enlightenment opened new questions, new fields, new forms of knowledge. The mysteries of the body, of magnetism, opened themselves to inquiring eyes. The revolution called forth visionaries. The revolutionaries not only saw more and farther: they were seen.

The revolution was seen as a series of spectacles, "such a scene."[7] The revolutionaries saw, and were seen. They saw themselves seen in the prints and paintings of the revolution. This was the gaze fulfilled, a *jouissance* of the sense of sight.

The exposure of the ancien regime was a festival of enlightenment and equality, stripping away the old concealments, the old illusions, the old trappings of pretentious authority. Burke saw as clearly as the sans-culottes that the nobility stood concealed behind "pleasing illusions . . . furnished from the wardrobe of a moral imagination." As he saw it, "all the decent drapery of life is to be rudely torn off," revealing "our naked shivering nature."[8] For Carlyle there was merit in the stripping away. "Shams are burnt up," he writes, "for it is the End of the dominion of IMPOSTURE."[9]

Opening the temples and stripping away the drapery revealed the equality of kings and people, but as Rousseau said of earlier revelations, the great thing is to make oneself believed. Behind the egalitarian violence of the revolution is a lapse of faith, a revolutionary apostasy, a lingering belief that there is power in the blood. The attacks on aristocrats, and the execution of the king, were directed at power in the flesh.

At the Temple, Louis Capet again confronted the words of the revolution, this time in the graffiti of his jailers. There was, among other things, a drawing of a guillotine, with the caption "Louis spitting in the sack."[10] Nor was he permitted the privileges of birth and blood. On the day of the execution, his valet was not permitted to cut his hair, for as the guard declared, "The executioner is good enough for him."[11] Another guard refused to deliver a package for him to his wife, saying, "That is no concern of mine. I am here to conduct you to the scaffold."[12] The concern with denying the signs of distinction to Louis Capet was also evident in the insistence on binding his hands. This act was read by Louis and his confessor as the most profound insult to his person. Certainly it marked a disavowal of royal inviolability.

Treatment of this sort was not, however, reserved to royals, or even to aristocrats. When Robespierre was lying wounded in the anteroom of the Committee on Public Safety, he was mocked in a fashion that called attention to both his former primacy and his evident humanity: "Oh Sire! is your Majesty in pain?"[13] Those who observed the scene remembered that he had had to wipe the blood from his mouth with little bits of paper and that his stockings had fallen about his ankles, small marks of humiliation that remind the reader of Robespierre's humanity.

There is, however, more to the violence of the French Revolution than the revelation of an all too visible humanity. The high are brought low, the mysteries of authority are revealed, and in the revelation destroyed, but violence, as Nietzsche observed, does not simply destroy, it establishes. Nietzsche asks, "How can one create a memory for the human animal?" and answers, "Man could never do without blood, torture, and sacrifices when he felt the need to create a memory for himself . . . pain is the most powerful aid to mnemonics." Violence, he writes, is essential to those promises by which men bind themselves to one another in politics.[14]

Freud's myth of primal rebellion, which so illuminates the role of violence in the establishment of identity, is particularly appropriate to a consideration of French revolutionary regicide.[15] For (let us give Filmer his due) what is the killing of a king if not the killing of the father?

It is reported in some histories, and many myths, that after Louis Capet's head was cut off, bystanders tasted the blood. His jailers had earlier written on the walls of the prison, "We're going to put up the big pig of the regime."[16] It is not necessary to see Louis as an edible, to see Louis consumed, to recognize in his execution the enactment of a totem meal. Aristocrats served, and were served, likewise. Foucault observed that rumor had it that "debauched aristocrats abducted little children to slaughter them and regenerate themselves by bathing in their blood." As Le Gaufey observed in the same exchange, "The vampire is always an aristocrat, and the saviour a bourgeois."[17] Sansculottes boasted of eating the hearts of aristocrats.

There were those, Robespierre knew (for he was among them), who would read in the rending of Louis Capet's body not the making but the rending of the body politic. In killing and consuming Louis and the aristocrats, the people of France absorbed their sovereignty. They disinterred the kings of France and laid them in a common grave, mingling their ashes not only with one another's but with those of the people. They came to comprehend in their collective character the authority that had once resided, hidden, in the bodies of the kings, and the sacred body of Saint Louis. In opening those bodies they opened the hidden places; they revealed the title held in blood to the gaze of all. In consuming those bodies, in mingling their ashes in a common grave, they incorporated the sovereignty these persons once possessed and buried it among the people. They incorporated the divine right of their kings.

Robespierre, arguing before the convention for the death of Louis, saw the possibility of a revisionist history, and a change in regime that might "even, perhaps, treat faithful friends of liberty as *cannibals,* as anarchists, as factious men."[18] Images of cannibalism haunted the revolution. A dissenting deputy described the National Assembly as "this cavern of Anthropophages."[19]

"I knew," Burke writes, "that the sufferings of monarchs make a delicious repast to some sort of palates," but he is horrified to see their bodies serve similarly.[20] Accepting the veracity of the *Times* correspondents, he wrote of the revolutionaries "devouring as a nutriment of their ferocity some part of the bodies of those they have murdered; their drinking the blood of their victims." Burke, like the editor of *Revolutions de Paris,* recognized that the people had become "mangeur de rois."[21] Carlyle, generations later, would write of "Catholicism, Classicism, Sentimentalism, Cannibalism: all isms that make up Man in France."[22]

For other Britons, the cannibalism of the sans-culottes was a more savage totem feast. James Gillray pictured *Dumourier Dining in State at St James on the 15th of May, 1793* served up with the severed head of the king. *Un Petit Souper à la Parisienne* showed a sans-culotte at table, delicately detaching an eyeball as a baby is basted on the spit.

The British had no taste for this supper; they had eaten earlier. Consider, Carlyle writes, the contemporary reports "there is on record a Trial of Charles First! This printed *Trial of Charles First* is sold and read everywhere at present—*quelle spectacle!* Thus did the English People judge their Tyrant, and become the first of Free Peoples."[23]

Flesh was not, however, to be the food of the French for long. They, like the British, would not need to kill another king. Other kings, even emperors, could be deposed and sent into exile. The opening of the king's body or the mixing of royal ashes in a common grave accomplished the ends at which they aimed. Authority flowed out to the people. Words replaced blood as the medium of authority.

The death of the king, was not vengeance, it was not even lèse-majesté. Regicide testified to an imperfect faith in a common humanity. The regicide French had, like Thomas, to stick a finger in the wound. Regicide followed upon the desire to believe in an equality that remained not quite believable. The act marked a failure of nerve.

"It remains to be seen," Carlyle observed, how the "sacred right of Insurrection was blown away by gunpowder."[24]

The executions of their former lords had enabled citizens to lay claim, psychologically and semiotically, to the authority of the ancien regime. The structures of revolutionary violence, the machinery that prosecuted the Terror in the cities, the war on the borders and abroad, enabled the revolutionary regime to lay claim to that authority institutionally. The apparatus that conducted the Terror and promulgated the ideology of the revolution provided a set of institutions and procedures to take the place of those the revolution had made illegitimate.

Weber and Freud both provide accounts of the effects of the structure of the Church and the army.[25] The derivation of *clerk* from *cleric* contains an implicit genealogy that Weber's account of the rise of bureaucratic authority details. The structure of the Church provided the model, and the first functionaries, of Western bureaucracy. The application of the word *officer* to civil as well as military authorities, marks the kinship between these two forms of organization. The army, with its ranked hierarchy, its division into departments with specialized functions, and its semiotic identity with the nation gave its form to the structures of the bureaucracy.

Because the Church was essential to order in the ancien regime, its replacement was at once inevitable and impossible. The Church sanctioned, indeed consecrated, the rule of kings. For centuries, it had replicated in its form the hierarchy of the regime. The First Estate had voted with the Second. The nobility provided sons (younger sons) and daughters for positions of rule in the Church. The Church, in Richelieu and Mazarin, had provided rulers to the nobility. The ideology that sanctioned the division of nobles and commons was disseminated by the Church in its function as educator.

The success of the revolution depended on the displacement of the Church and on the appropriation of its authority and power. The amended prayers and litanies, the adapted rituals, of the revolutionaries appropriated the forms and structures of the Church. In doing so, they draw our attention to one of the ironies of the creation of revolutionary memory. The assimilated forms, invested with a new content, nevertheless remained to preserve not only the memory but the power of the Church. In adopting the forms of the Church the revolution placed itself under ecclesiastical authority. Those who thought to abridge the authority of the Church became the unwitting agents of its continuance.

It was likewise with the army. Danton, like so many others in revolutions then and since, looked to the army and to war abroad for the preservation of the revolution. It was not merely that he felt the revolution threatened, as it surely was, by the possibility of counterrevolutionary invasion and insurrection. He recognized that the army and the act of war provided both a material expression of the claim to sovereignty and the means to maintain it.

The army stands on the boundaries of the nation, to defend and to extend them. It is called by the name that is given to the nation, and serves as its representative in war and peace. The accouterments of an army—uniforms and medals, badges of rank, banners and flags—write this claim upon it. It acts in the name of the nation, as the embodiment of the general will. It is a mass of people formed into a single body that moves and acts with a single will, a model of the nation. It serves, as a sign and in its actions, to define the nation, giving it a material expression. In it the nation appears incarnate, willful, and active.

Warfare did not die with the nobility. As the nobility had acquired authority through the shedding of blood in war and the assumption of war as a calling, so too would the citizens. The call "Aux armes, citoyens! Formez vos bataillons" was the anthem of the new republic. That republic saw itself embodied in the citizen-soldier. In the early days of this revolution—as with so many—women marched, attacked, defended, fought, and died with men, and often in the vanguard. This was the force of the people assembled. As the irregular forces of the revolution give way to the regular army, disciplined and hierarchical, of the state, the army is made masculine.

The process of centralization that had been advanced by the army in the years before the revolution was accelerated in the revolutionary mobilizations. The army itself provided a model for bureaucratic organization, now refined by the elimination of considerations of birth in promotion. This model was disseminated by the expansion of the army and by the *levée en masse,* which sought to involve all citizens in the military effort. Perhaps more important, however, were the structures that developed for the provisioning of the army. The size of the expanded army and the pressure on the government to keep food available at reasonable prices to a restive population made the efficient organization of the process of provisioning a political necessity. The structures and procedures developed in this massive undertaking survived the fall of the republic to serve the empire.

The model of the army was not well suited to the ideology of the revolution. As with the Church, the forms that the revolutionaries sought to fill with a new content retained their old authority. The form of the army inscribed on the emerging regime a system of hierarchy altogether at odds with the ideology of the revolution. Whatever their virtues, armies are not the province of liberty, equality, or fraternity. They replicate in their form the elaborate systems of rank and hierarchy that marked the ancien regime. Claims to military conquest, and the possession of armies, had given the French nobility the title to rule. In the army, as among the nobility, power followed the flow of blood.

Both the Church and the army, Freud notes, are institutions with a single head, "who loves all the individuals in the group with an equal love," or, in Foucault's more sinister description, "looms over everything with a single gaze."[26] The community of the Church and the comradeship of the army come in consequence of the bond with the leader, whether Christ or commander in chief. This leader, according to Freud, is (like a king) like a father. The Church and the army oblige their followers to look for identity and authority in a single person. They tie the sense of community, of fraternity, among their members to the acclamation of a single leader. In appropriating the forms and functions of the Church and the army, the revolutionaries preserved the memory, and the institutions, of the ancien regime, and invited in the emperor.

Writing and violence are bound together in Napoleon. Whether he is remembered as general and emperor or as the Little Corporal, he was a soldier, a man who came to rule through acts of violence. His title, like the titles of aristocrats, was given him through the flow of blood. Yet he left his most durable legacy not in the achievements of war but in the Code Napoléon. Napoleon, like his revolutionary predecessors, sought to transubstantiate blood into writing. With the Code Napoléon, an aristocracy of the blood yields its place to an aristocracy of the pen. Foucault also recognized Napoleon as a juncture, though of a slightly different sort. "The importance, in historical mythology, of the Napoleonic character probably derives from the fact that it is at the point of junction of the monarchical, ritual, exercise of sovereignty, and the hierarchical, permanent exercise of indefinite discipline."[27] Foucault's delineation recognizes the connection of the change in authority to a profound change in the economy of sight. In reading Napoleon as a juncture, Foucault marked him as the inauguration of an age.

Too much of authority was hidden in the past, too much is revealed at present, for this periodization to be altogether persuasive. Nor can Foucault's resonant reading account for the importance, at the time and in our memories, of the storming of the Bastille and the Declaration of Independence.

Neither the resurgence of the army and the Church nor the return of kings should be read as the death of the revolution. It is the end of the ancien regime that we remember in the revolution, not its brief resurgence afterward. Memory does not deceive us here. The revolution made in its time, and marks in ours, the end of one age and the beginning of another.

# 11
## The Death of Marat

In the memory of the French Revolution, the passage of authority from violence to writing is marked by the death of Marat. Not all executions released authority to the one who killed. Charlotte Corday's assassination of Marat with a table knife has all the makings of a totem meal, but she does not incorporate his authority. She opens his body, but his authority does not flow out to her. In the memory of Marat's assassination the revolution records the triumph of writing over blood.

The death of Marat is remembered not as Charlotte Corday's act but as David's painting (figure 11-1). The painting is a composition of extraordinary grace. In it David becomes the author of a text of great force and lucidity and the possessor of political authority. This painting is full of writing. It is not only the presence of the letter but its content that is called to our attention. The light falls full upon it; it can be easily read. On the rough table David has written "À Marat," as if to inscribe a monument, and signed it "David." The composition changes the viewer into reader, the painter into author.

The text of the painting is a forceful affirmation of Marat's continuing authority, and so a work with political authority of its own. In it David successfully resisted the moderate opposition to the Mountain, transforming Marat from a radical politician to a saint of the revolution. Representations of Marat filled Jacobin clubs and public buildings. His writings were granted a posthumous authority.

It is as a representation of the power of writing that Marat remains in the memory of the revolution. He figures in David's painting as

Figure 11-1. Jacques Louis David, *Marat at His Last Breath*, Museés Royales des Beaux Arts, Brussels, *Fort*, Luc de Nanteuil, *Jacques-Louis David* (New York: Harry Abrams 1985 colorplate 21).

author, and text. He retains his authority and becomes the occasion for David's.

For Carlyle, Marat wavers between the living and the dead, the visible and the invisible, the word and flesh. The name Marat gives his paper, *L'Ami du peuple,* becomes his name. The pamphlets he authors become his material manifestation. One can "hardly believe there is a Marat, except in print." He is a "Spectrum, swart unearthly visual appearance." When he manifests himself in the flesh before the Convention, it is as "the Bodily Spectrum of People's-Friend Marat. Shriek ye Seven hundred and Forty-nine."

> Marat is no phantasm of the brain, or mere lying impress of Printer's Types; but a thing material, of joint and sinew, and a certain small stature; ye behold him there, in his blackness, in his dingy squalor, a living fraction of Chaos and Old Night; visibly incarnate, desirous to speak.[1]

In Marat the word was made flesh, and the flesh made legible. He is remembered as the man marked by a rather horrible disease of the skin. It must be a rare account that does not call attention to Marat's disease. His skin was peeling away. Forced underground, he had contracted the disease in the sewers of Paris. The revolution and his own persecution had left their mark on him. His commitment to the revolution was legible on his person as in his writings. He was, Carlyle writes, "ill of Revolution Fever."[2] Even before his death, he was a man who had become a text.

The peculiar character of Marat's disease alters the meaning of the assassination. Marat's subjection to the vicissitudes of the flesh was all too evident, his humanity all too tangible. The act of violence that reveals humanity by opening the body was, in Marat's case, a superfluity, for his body had already been opened before the eyes of the people.

The death of Marat, in the memory of the French Revolution, marks the triumph of writing over violence, of ink over blood. Marat marks the transition from traditional to rational legal legitimacy. Like an aristocrat, his authority is in his person. Unlike the aristocrat, he derives his distinction from writing rather than from blood. The representations of his death affirm that the capacity for authority, to rule in inscriptions, survives death by violence. Death belongs to the flesh and to the feminine.

The painting shows Marat marked by Corday. The knife lies abandoned in the foreground. There is a small wound on his chest, blood stains the water of the bath a vivid crimson. Marat is shown in death, but he has not lost his authority. The green baize of his improvised writing table is thrown over the bath, hiding most of the blood. The wound is deeply shadowed. Marat's hand still holds a pen; paper and ink are on a rough table beside him. His assassin appears in a letter. She comes to him as a petitioner comes, another mark of his authority. The text of the letter reads "Du 13 Juillet 1793 Marie Anne Charlotte Corday au Citoyen *Marat*. Il suffit que je sois bien malheureuse pour avoir Droit à votre bienveillance."[3] Marat's thumb—indeed, the line of his body from his head to his arm—points to the final word, *bienveillance*. Corday places herself under Marat's eye, in his sight. It is only in this letter, where she remains in his sight, in his power, that she is in the painting at all.

Long after the revolution, after Napoleon, after the restoration of the Bourbons, the scene of Marat's last breath would be painted from an altered perspective. In Baudry's painting (figure 11-2) it is Corday who dominates the composition. Marat, in the pose made famous by David, is seen from a less attractive perspective. The knife is in the wound. Corday stands as if she still wielded it, her hand clenched. She is placed before a map of France, as if in her France had become flesh. All the other writing in the room—Marat's work—is in disarray. In this painting, responsive, imitative, one sees how thoroughly David had established the terms in which Marat's death was understood. Baudry attempted to recall a moment of bloodshed, of a woman's triumph, evidence of the primacy of the body. But as Rousseau observed, "the great thing is to make oneself believed." David's Marat had already become the icon of a secular ascension.

In David's painting, Marat is writing and written; the woman is the emptiness at the center. Marat is shown "at his last breath," still living, surrounded by, and embedded in, the writing that will ensure his transcendence, his body inscribed. The absence of Charlotte Corday shows her in flight, unarmed. She is not the victor nor the assassin; she is a fugitive. In this moment, the woman as subject, the woman's power, is erased. In David's painting, as in Rousseau's philosophy, woman becomes the absence upon which all else depends.

David's painting, like Rousseau's philosophy, predicates the triumph of writing on the absent woman. In her absence, Corday the triumphant assassin is read in her traces as petitioner and fugitive. In David's work, as in Rousseau's, the woman, victorious in the body, is defeated through words.

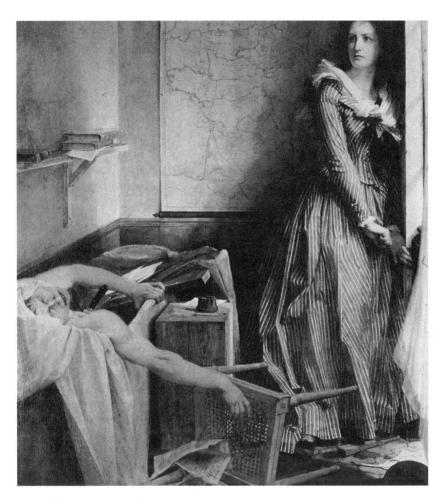

Figure 11-2. Paul Baudry, *The Death of Marat.*

David had argued for the authority of fathers over mothers, of men over women, in *Brutus* and *The Oath of the Horatii.* In *The Oath of the Horatii* the sons stand, swords upraised, before the father, a band of brothers subsumed in his name, obedient to his word. The women, mother and daughters, sisters and wives, are seated, leaning on one another in a huddled mass. There are no marks of hierarchy or authority among them; they are alike in their exclusion from power. In *Brutus* the father receives the dead bodies of the sons he had condemned to death for conspiring against the Roman republic for the return of monarchy. The women and the dead bodies of the sons form a backdrop of light against which Brutus and the dark statue of Roma are set. Enlightenment displays the failure of the flesh. Monarchy, maternal power, and familial bonds are counterposed to the republic, law, and the stoic allegiance of the individual citizen. Authority belongs to Brutus, father and statesman, who, like a republican Chronos, has devoured his children. In *The Death of Marat* we confront the authority not of the surviving father but of the dead son. The power of the word is the means to an apotheosis.

David's painting of Marat conjoins political with aesthetic radicalism. The work marks a radical departure from the tenets of Rococo painting. Le Brun's canonical handbook "insisted that facial expression was the principle means of representing the passions."[4] The Académie not only emphasized facial expression (of a severely stylized sort) in its pedagogy, it also reserved a particularly prestigious award for the preeminent "tête d'expression." David, in common with his fellow Jacobins, recognized the need to remove, if not the privileged heads, at least the privilege from the heads. Rather than give primacy to facial expression, David elaborated a vivid gestural vocabulary in which not only the face, but the body as a whole was to be read. "This dramatic aesthetic revolution, which made a lasting and indelible impression on French art, privileged the entire body over the head."[5] Dorothy Johnson ascribes this "revolutionary corporal aesthetic" to Diderot, who wrote "il y a des gestes sublime que toute l'éloquence oratoire ne rendra jamais."[6] Diderot may well have been the principal philosophic influence on David. It is Rousseau, however, whose account of gesture most illumines David's work.

Gesture, Rousseau argues in *On the Origin of Language,* is the first, most economical, and most eloquent, language. Yet gesture, the language of passion, will be overcome, first by the language of need, then by pictographs and ideograms, and finally by alphabetic language, the language of universalism and modernity.[7] Gesture, for Rousseau, is on the way to language. Writing is already present within it. Gesture marks the primacy of the eye over the ear, the hand over the mouth, writing over speech.

In David's painting of Marat, all the visceral intensity, all the power of the silent speech of gesture, is placed in the service of the word. The painting exploits the communicative power of gesture to show the failure of the flesh and the power of the surviving word. Marat's body is the body of submission, the supine body of the Christian Passion. This is the body vulnerable, the body in pain, the body sacrificed. On this body is written the failed power of the flesh.

The dead bodies of revolutionary heros, like the dead bodies of Christian martyrs in an earlier iconography, were bodies to be read.

The insistent visual reiteration of their infirmities, the instruments of their torture and death, testified to the power of the word and the inauguration of a new order.

Marat died by a woman's hand. The association of death with feminine sexuality does not end with that. Many have spoken of the femininity of Marat's body in this painting, yet this body is visibly the body of a man. The figure's femininity derives not from its form but from the composition. Marat's body is feminine in its pose, in its openness, not in its anatomy. The signs that commonly tell us the body's gender are superseded here. The marks written on the face are overwritten by the turban and the open mouth; the marks of gender on the chest and arms are overwritten with the sign of the woman's sex.

David painted the dying Marat in the classic position of the odalisque: open, unclothed, supine. Turbaned in a towel, the mouth half open, Marat's head might be that of a figure from a seraglio. The intense eroticism of this portrait derives from the reiteration of Marat's openness: Eastern and feminine. This is the body of desire: the desired and desiring body, the penetrated body of the colonized. This is a body open to Charlotte Corday and opened by her, lying with open arms in the open mouth of the bath, marked with an open wound, inscribed with the woman's sex. The signs of an interrupted intercourse are transliterated into the signs of death: the rumpled sheet, the pen falling from the hand. The death of Marat makes the signs of the feminine and the erotic evocative of death.

Women serve as the icon of death in several of David's history paintings. Light, and a composition that places them on the same plane, links the mourning women of *Brutus* with the headless and impotent bodies of the defeated sons. The women of *The Oath of the Horatii* mourn the death about to fall upon the Horatii and Curatii. Andromache sits in mourning before the body of Hector.[8] The woman at the center of *The Anger of Achilles* is the distant occasion for his imminent death. In *Antiochus and Stratonice,* the brightly lit Stratonice is the innocent cause of impending death. Andromache, Stratonice, Iphigenia, and the wife of Brutus are presented to the gaze. They are brightly lit, they draw the eye, yet they are clothed. In all these paintings, and elsewhere throughout his work, David couples the naked bodies of dead and dying men with the clothed bodies of living women. The open wounds, the visible death of the men, is counterposed to the hidden sex of the women. The visible wounds and naked bodies of men become exchangeable for the hidden feminine erotic.

The exchange of the visible wound for the hidden sex, of masculine death for feminine sexuality, inverts Freud's account of the fetish. In David's paintings, the wound is visible, the sex is hidden. The visible wound serves to mark—and disavow—the woman's sex. What is sited by Freud and by David, is not simply masculine or feminine, power or lack, but the *unheimlich,* unspeakable aporias that bracket our corporeal existence. The wound and the woman's sex are the signs and sites of the openness that must be closed, the gates that lead away from bodily integrity. The fetish, in the Freudian account, marks the aporia as lack, as impotence, as the danger of losing oneself in the other. David's paintings inscribe the bodies of dead men with the seductive power of the hidden erotic and the promise of death's uncertainty.

In "Marat" there is no woman and no death. The woman is there no longer and death has not yet come. Marat is shown, in David's words, "à son dernier soupir." Marat at his last breath is still living, surrounded by, and embedded in, the writing that will ensure his transcendance. The eroticism of David's painting of Marat, the exchange of a man's wounds for a woman's sex, appears in several of his paintings. In his paintings of heroic antiquity, the heavily draped bodies of mourning women called up the deaths they mourned. Their erotic ties to the dead, dying, or doomed heroes were conflated with death. In his paintings of revolutionary heros, women disappear. Only the dead or wounded body of the hero is visible. Anatole Devosges's portrait drawing *Michel Lepeletier de Saint-Fargeau on His Deathbed* echoes the text of David's Marat. The sheets are in disarray, the head is thrown back, and a sword (with the head of a cock) is poised to penetrate the body. Like David's *The Death of Marat,* the drawing affirms the primacy of writing and the demise of the authority of the body. The body—open, feminine, dying—is the body of an aristocrat; the sword—Gallic and phallic—is linked to the written word.

In David's portrait of the martyred Joseph Bara, Thomas Crow observed, "The sensuality of the body goes beyond a beauty appropriate to its age and innocence."[9] Crow is exact. This body might be the body of a woman or a girl, and its sensuality altogether conventional. The subject, however, is not a sleeping woman but a martyred boy. The masculine sensuality of the pose depends upon the inscription of death upon it. The portraits of Marat and Lepeletier derive their openness from their wounds. The portrait of Bara uses the signs of sexual openness to evoke the wound David conceals.

The heroic portraits of Marat, Bara, and Lepeletier are portraits of men who achieve an apotheosis after death in the order of the written law. In Gericault's *Heads of the Executed* (figure 11-3), two victims of the guillotine lie, again, on rumpled sheets. One, perhaps a woman, certainly more feminine, might be asleep; the absence of the body is concealed by the sheet. The older man's severed head is clearly shown, his eyes and mouth open. The guillotined achieve no apotheosis here. The open body is the dead body; its eroticism translated into fear.

Gustave Courbet's *L'Origine du monde* (figure 11-4) offers an ironic commentary on the eroticism assigned the open body, seizing it and attaching it to its referent. Here the open body, sex visible and inviting, is unambiguously feminine, yet it lacks a head. The image of the guillotined, invested by the revolution with the erotic power of open transgression, returns here to invest the woman's body with an erotic and dangerous power.[10] Courbet's painting, as Lacan recognized, is what it claims to be: a portrait of the origin of the world. The centrality of sex, the identification of sexuality and irrationality, openness and trans-

Figure 11-3. Gericault, *Heads of the Executed,* National Museum, Stockholm, Dorinda Outram, *The Body and the French Revolution* (New Haven: Yale University Press 1989), 121.

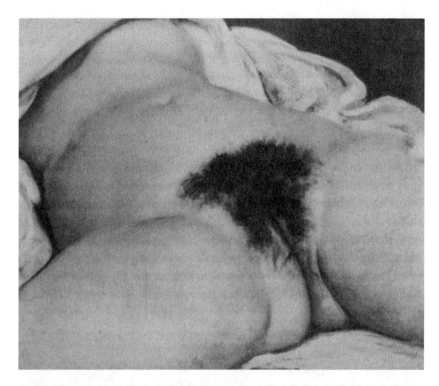

Figure 11-4. Gustave Courbet, *L'Origine du monde,* Musée d'Orsay, Jorg Zutter and Petra ten Doesschate-Chu, *Courbet* (Paris: Flammarion, 1998).

gression, and the location of all these in woman's body are conditions present in the site of our origins.

The popular iconography of the French Revolution inscribed the erotic power of feminine sexuality on the images and instruments of revolutionary death, but it also transformed the feminine sex from the site where life is created to the site where life is extinguished.

It was in the feminine, as *la guillotine,* that the instrument of a humane death entered the language. She would also be called "Petite-Louison" and "Louisette," sister to "the maiden" in Scotland. The femininity of the guillotine was reiterated in the preoccupation with feminine victims, feminine observers. Mme. Elizabeth appeals to modesty, Charlotte Corday blushes, Mme. Roland and Mme. Capet go to a common death, and Dickens's Madame Defarge knits like a Fate at the foot of the scaffold, recording without writing. The guillotine was a feminine site: the site of the deaths of women, of deaths in women's sight, of deaths authored by women.

The guillotine, assigned a series of feminine nicknames by the French, took on feminine sexual attributes in the images of the English. George Cruikshank's *A Radical Reformer* (figure 11-5) represents the guillotine as a (male) sans-culotte, but this sans-culotte has not a phallus but a bleeding hole. Within that hole, lest the point escape the viewer, a tiny head can be seen. The guillotine was the instrument, to the uneasy English, of *fureur utérine:* indiscriminate, uncontrolled, open to all, bringing all settled certainties, all hierarchies, into doubt. The guillotine was the instrument of irrationality, severing the head. As the condemned lost their heads and the executioner held up the now silent, unspeaking mouth, another mouth appeared below it, unspeaking and unspeakable. Thus Mme. Elizabeth "pleaded with the executioner to replace the scarf covering her neck "au nom de pudeur."[11] In opening the body, the guillotine made all feminine: silent, irrational, impotent, open, subject.

The body of the executed became the site of uncertainty, aporia, speculation. The femininity of these bodies entailed not only a physical but a conceptual openness. They were questionable. Could they

Figure 11-5. George Cruikshank, *A Radical Reformer*, 1819, Richard Vogler George Cruikshank Collection. Los Angeles, figure 8, p.61 in *French Caricature and the French Revolution, 1789–1799,* Grunewald Center for the Graphic Arts, Wight Art Gallery, University of California, Los Angeles, published in conjunction with an exhibit organized by the University of California, Los Angeles, and the Bibliotheque nationale de France, Paris, 1989.

feel? Could they see? What could they conceive? What would come of them? Surely they were impotent, yet they might also prove themselves miraculous. "I am convinced," Soemmering wrote, "that if air continued to pass regularly through the vocal organs, and if these organs had not been destroyed, the heads would speak."[12] The heads were now possessed, like women, of mouths that never could speak. The open bodies of the guillotined, like the open body of woman, were insufficient and excessive, unspeaking and unspeakable, beyond the reach of reason, beyond language.

The closed body had a head that could think and speak, and therefore declare with Descartes, "Cogito ergo sum." The open body of the executed had, as Arasse noted, silently answered the enlightenment, "I think, but I am not." "The guillotine slices in half the reassurance of the Cartesian cogito."[13] After the guillotine, the modern, postrevolutionary subject is not only shaped by the Enlightenment but "bears like a flatfish, the traces of having been cut in two."[14]

# 12
## The Perverse Authority of Writing

The daring of Sade was not in doing (there was no novelty in that) but in putting the unspeakable (or, rather, the unspoken) into words. Deleuze writes that "in principle, violence is something that does not speak, or speaks but little."[1] Violence speaks. Violence speaks not out of the body but onto it, in it, not to the ear alone, but to hearing, sight, and touch. Writing is the language of sight, speech that of hearing. Violence uses these languages, but it depends upon the language of touch, an impassioned braille. Violence writes on the body, it elicits a cry, and it speaks through pain—and pleasure. Sade's crime, and Sade's radicalism, lay not in speaking through violence but in speaking of it, in putting the speech of violence into words. The revolution had translated words into violent acts, and violent acts into words. Sade's transgression was speaking of the unspeakable. It was a revolutionary transgression: in it he joined the old regime to the new. For Sade, as for the revolution, authority moved from the flow of blood to the flow of words.

The ascendancy of the word in Sade puts the Enlightenment faith in the liberating power of language in question. In Sade's scenarios language serves not to free but to compel. Speech is not the medium of consent but the means to compulsion. Speech serves, not to replace violence, but to incite and enhance it.

Sade presents himself, in writing, as the spawn of the old regime and the author of the new. When Eugénie, heroine of *Philosophy in the Bedroom,* becomes a partisan of libertinage, she joins herself to an egalitarian community in which a gardener is as good as a chevalier. Sade's philosophers of the bedroom are partisans of the Enlightenment, deprecating those who still "vegetate in a superstitious twilight" and declaring that "all man-made laws which contravene Nature's are made for naught but our contempt."[2]

Throughout the work, Sade concurs in Hobbes's judgment that "every mother is a lord." "Dread not infanticide" Mme. de Sainte-Ange tells Eugénie, "the crime is imaginary: we are always mistress of what we carry in our womb." After birth, "we should still have the right to destroy it. In all the world there is no prerogative more secure than that of mothers over their children." Dolmance, another partisan of the open body, agrees, "The right is natural . . . it is incontestable." Yet Eugénie's rebellious libertinage is climaxed when she joins in sewing up her aristocratic mother's sex.[3]

In Sade's tract, a transgressive liberty takes the form of an assault on an aristocratic lineage, maternity, and feminine sexuality. Nature, in Sade's account, ranges the rights and power of the mother against the desires and growing power of her children. As the regicide republicans opened the body of the king, Sade sought to close off the bodies of women, whose title to rule followed from the procreative powers of their open bodies. The aristocrat's blood is shed, those who once dominated are forced to submit, a body open to pleasure is closed by pain, the mother's rule over her child is ended, and the possibility of reproduction is closed off.[4]

Sade, however, is no partisan of closure. Where he closes one orifice, he opens several others in its place. The coupling of phallus and vagina is replaced, in Sade's work, by the coupling of hand and eye. The hand writes those words that will penetrate the eye. The eye is entered and aroused. Phallologocentrism finds no more adept practitioner than Sade.

Sade anticipated Derrida's recognition of the autoeroticism of writing. The hand takes up the pen and writes; the reader's hand writes Sade's text on the receptive body. The privileged orifice is the reading eye, receiving the words the pen disseminates. Like Derrida, Sade writes over speech. The mouth becomes a place of entry rather than utterance. The mouth is not the site of self-expression but a place through which another enters. Hand and phallus have authority; the mouth is silent.

Pornography is proof enough that the triumph of the word does not displace the flesh. The modern, scriptural, literary body can be aroused by words, by marks on a page, by spoken words. Sade, Sade's readers, Sade's followers, and Sade's enemies are all people of the text. The letter, the word, the inscription on the page touch without touching. The word calls up the absent flesh. The voyeur becomes lover and loved, the reading eye becomes the aroused genitals. Sade's passionate exploitation of the economy of exchange upon which pornography depends extends beyond the effect of transubstantiation to exchanges of one word, one body part, for another.

Sade's perverse exchange of anus for vulva is, as Sade continually claimed, particularly consistent with the revolution. This is libertinage in the service of equality. Michelet, in his history of France, marked the anus as the site of equality. Recording an anal affliction of the autocratic Louis XIV, he writes, "While he saw himself painted on the ceilings of Versailles as more than a man, a sun of youth, beauty and vitality this brazen nature was telling him: 'You are a man.' Nature permitted herself to take him in the place where all men are humiliated." The infirmity transformed Louis from king to man, from man to the form of a woman violated. Resisting treatment, attempting to contain a secret that "could not fail to burst all bounds," Louis feared—"not without reason—that Europe would laugh, and would take courage by such laughter."[5] The passage, in which Roland Barthes saw only "black blood," makes the anus exchangeable with the woman's sex. Michelet identifies the open body of the king with the violation and impregnation of a woman. "Nine whole months he resisted," containing the secret within him. The opening of his body, the revelation of the secret is, like the revelation of Baubo, the occasion for democratic—and subversive—laughter.

This is the sex of fraternity. Marked as masculine, it lays claim to universality. Even gender distinctions are erased in anality, Hocquengham argued, for everyone has an anus. Taking this orifice under one's control, disciplining it, making it responsive to one's will in obedience to social conventions, is the price of entry into the social order. The acquisition of sociality and individuality are simultaneous. The understanding of the anal as that which one must keep to oneself, as that which must remain private, secures the boundaries as it disciplines the behavior of the individual. "The functions of this organ are truly private. . . . The anus expresses privatisation itself."[6] This is the metaphoric, and libidinal, site of private property. Hocquengham's recognition of the link between capitalism and the anal follows from Freud's identification of the anal as the realm of artificial value, of money. Deleuze and Guattari, following Freud, write, "The first organ to be privatised, to be excluded from the social field, was the anus. It gave privatisation its model, just as money was expressing the new abstract status of the fluxes."[7] This is the site of an unnatural production. This is the site of privatization and theatricality, of a spectacular commerce, of dramatic artifice and artificial value. This is the realm of the rational actor. This is the perverse cathexis of an emerging capitalism.

All the institutions most characteristic of a rational order have their perverse equivalents in Sade: the school and the prison, the Church and the army. There is not only philosophy in the bedroom, there is instruction in the parlor, and all with the appropriate scholastic accompaniments. Colleagues prompt disquisitions with pretended questions, offer critiques, collaborate, and put forward alternative schema. Students are chided ("Eugénie, you are forgetting your lessons"), strive for consistency ("In accordance with the maxims wherewith I am inculcated here"), question their professors ("Would you not like to persuade me, dear teachers, that you have never done what you have conceived?"), show promise ("Ah! What a mind!"), and surpass their teachers ("Excellent idea indeed! It does you honor, my dear; it would never have occurred to me").[8] Victims are tried, sent to confinement by lettres de cachet, detained, tortured, imprisoned, and released. Mme. de Mistival, for example, is sent to be detained and tortured by a letter from her husband. There are prayers and ejaculations, carefully choreographed liturgies and rituals. There are initiates and novices, and the disciplines and maxims by means of which the latter become the former. Violence is ordered here. One advances in the ranks through knowledge, experience, and courage under fire. One's rank is determined not merely by birth but by natural attributes and performance.

Like the Jacobins, Sade is a rebel against the Church. Like the Jacobins (and unlike the Jacobins), Sade is concerned with corruption. Like the Jacobins (and unlike the Jacobins), Sade sees the passing of an age. The Jacobins, in their preoccupation with corruption, in their rending and their ravaging, in their passion for disorder and a new order, in their impiety and their piety, are ranged with an earlier reformer, and an earlier eschatology. "I am a ripe shit," Luther declared, "and the world is a great ass-hole. I think we will let go of each other soon enough."[9] Sade wanted to get back in.

The exchange of the anus for the vulva as the privileged site of sexual intercourse identifies the open body not only with things coming into being but with their necessary passing away. Burke saw the Jacobins as the agents of this passage, "dephlegmated, defecated evil" who, flying high, "souse down upon our tables and leave nothing unrent, unrifled, unravaged, or unpolluted with the slime of their filthy offal." Not simply nature on a rampage, but the rampant, unthinking production and dissemination of artificial value. Burke feared not nature on a rampage but a rampaging order naturalized.[10]

Sade's passion for liberty, his misogyny, and his desire to close off the feminine body echo the Jacobins. Yet Sade remains a figure of the old regime, a marquis. Sade is an aristocrat, using sexuality and the shedding of blood as means to domination, taking pleasure in rule. The figure of Sade, aristocratic, dominating, sexual, opposes itself to democracy, self-government, self-control, and the closed body of the Incorruptible Robespierre. Marat's erotic, open body is the body of death and a rational, scriptural transcendence. Sade's erotic, open body is the entry into madness.

The oppositions—writing and sexuality, writing and madness— coupled in these figures animate Peter Weiss's play *The Persecution and Assassination of Jean-Paul Marat as Performed by the Inmates of the Asylum of Charenton Under the Direction of the Marquis de Sade*. The play touches an anxiety at the center of the revolution, of liberalism, of modernity. Marat's writing enables him to transcend the body. Writing can overcome the shedding of blood, the death of the body. Sexuality remains. Sade's writing serves not to transcend but to extend and intensify bodily sensation. Sade's writing seems not the instrument of order but a vessel for madness. *Marat/Sade* reveals the shape of an abyss: the presence of madness, transgression, and the body in the rationality, order, and abstraction of writing, and the presence of obedience in transgression. Sade came to preoccupy late moderns not merely because of his trangressive sexuality but because of his transgressive writing.[11]

The most effective testimony to the ending of Sade's age comes from Sade's later and lesser epigones. In the work of William Burroughs, in *L'histoire d'O* and other such, pious rituals of sexual transgression are presented as credentials for literary distinction. An already institutionalized misogyny is presented as transgression. These partisans of the naive obscene misunderstand their own allegiances. That which they take for transgression affirms an already established order. That which they take to be an affirmation of sexuality, of the body, of the "belly-to-belly tension between man and woman" (or man and man) is an affirmation not of the power of the body but of the power of writing. The defense of obscenity, because it is in writing, because it has literary value, is a literary faith and has literary disciples.

Bataille, in a view that Deleuze endorses, argued that Sade's language "is essentially that of a victim." Torturers use the language of authority and order; victims employ the language of violence. "The violent man is willing to keep quiet and connives at cheating."[12] For Deleuze—as for Bataille—this honesty gives Sade an absolution. Bataille's text "ought to invalidate all theories linking Sade to Nazism."[13] Much turns, for Bataille and Deleuze, on the silence of the violent. If "only the victim can describe torture," then Sade's fulsome descriptions of the pleasures of pain belong to the liberating project of the Enlightenment. Sade becomes a scientist. Are scientists so innocent?

In Sade's works the word imposes itself on the body, the letter ruptures the boundary between the living and the dead. In Sade's scenes, discourse serves authority. Reason serves not to free everyone but to force some to submit. Insofar as we are under the authority of the word, pornography can give pleasure (or pain). Those who authorize the policies and sign the orders that issue in torture and disappearance can be held as culpable as those who carry out the acts on the flesh of their common victims. In this sense (but only in this sense) Deleuze can affirm that "reasoning itself is a form of violence" and "the acts of violence performed on the victims are a mere reflection of a higher form of violence to which the demonstration testifies."[14] Deleuze argues:

> The libertine may put on an act of trying to convince and persuade; he may even proselytize and gain new recruits (as in *Philosophy in the Bedroom*). But the intention to convince is merely apparent, for nothing is more alien to the sadist than the wish to convince, to persuade, in short, to educate. . . . He is not even attempting to prove anything to anyone.[15]

Sade's libertine may be putting on an act, but he is a rational actor. The pretense of persuasion serves the interest of domination. For Deleuze, instruction and education, persuasion and domination, compulsion and consent remain distinct. Sade saw the presence of the instructor in the educator, the presence of the desire to dominate in the intention to convince, the presence of compulsion in consent.

Sade thus reveals a threat to the liberatory pretenses of the proponents of communicative subjectivity. For the partisans of communicative action, equal individuals present themselves to each other in language and find—or make—common ground. In Sade's work, adepts instill desires in their initiates that bind the initiates to them. The field of language serves domination rather than liberation, hierarchy rather than equality. Reason serves not to free but to compel, for inscribed within it is the imperative of necessity. Those one overcomes with the language of reason are forced to obey. If they later discover better reasons, what then? The matter is closed. The language of reason shows itself in Sade as a means for the imposition of one's desire on an unwilling other.

"The sadist is in need of institutions, the masochist of contractual relations."[16] Sade's text demonstrates the presence of domination in persuasion. Masoch's, as Deleuze recognized, demonstrates the presence of compulsion in contract. "The middle ages," Deleuze writes, "distinguished with considerable insight between two types of commerce with the devil: the first resulted from possession, the second from a pact of alliance."[17] Deleuze wishes to preserve the distinction between institutions and contracts, domination and persuasion. The practices of our time answer that contracts create institutions and institutions proliferate contracts.

Sade has the last word in libertinage. Sacher-Masoch announces the authority of the word that governs the body, the cathexis and the conundrums of contract.[18] The text of *Venus in Furs* is replete with contracts. Here contract appears not as the overcoming of slavery but as its replacement. As Wanda regrets the passage of slavery, Severin declares, "I want your power over me to become law." "And what if I should take you at your word?" Wanda asks. She draws up a contract, refuses to negotiate its provisions, and declares, "You can no longer lay claim to any rights, and there is no limit to my power over you."[19] Severin becomes a slave in signing this contract. Yet it is through this complete abjection that he has the proofs of love, for any mark of affection from the holder of absolute power is, of necessity, freely given. In Sacher-Masoch's contractarian world, the exercise of volition, the freedom of the will, is evident only in the exercise of absolute power, or the submission to slavery. Sacher-Masoch speaks, as Deleuze recognized, to the cathexis of contract—and to its contradictions.

# Section 4

# 13
## Sacrifice

Those who undertook to condemn Charles Stuart and Louis Capet were acutely conscious that they sat in judgment not on particular men but on systems of right and sovereignty. With those deaths, more than a person was cast into oblivion.[1] Yet the death of monarchy came through the death of the person who embodied that system—the end of aristocracy through the ending of aristocrats. Those who carried the title to rule in their bodies, in the blood, surrendered that title in the same form. "No man can reign innocently," Saint Just argued.[2] Guilt attached not only to the system in the abstract but to those who were its particular incarnation. Fanon's *The Wretched of the Earth* commended violence as Saint Just had, but recognized, as Saint Just had not, that the seeming symmetry of regicide and Terror—attacking the bodies of those who claimed to rule in the body—was undone by the semiotics of exchange that sanctioned it.

The capacity of violence to put an end not only to particular lives but to a political order was reaffirmed in the struggles that would end colonial rule. Here too, as Saint Just had declared to an earlier revolutionary age, "The Revolution begins when the tyrant ends."[3] Yet in the colonized nations, authority could not be severed with a head. The sword and the guillotine were partly, but only partly, successful. Through them, the bodies of the kings had been opened and power flowed out to the people. Authority, power, and privilege, once centered in the body of the king, had been disseminated. The sacrifice of kings and aristocrats brought an end to monarchy and aristocracy, but it did not bring an end to rule in the body.

We have been haunted, we unknowing ones, by the arrogant imposition of this all too partial closure. Like the sons who kill and consume the father only to find him alive within them, we have found the voice of the dead difficult to still within us. Having put an end to the ruler in the flesh had not put an end to rule in the flesh, nor to the rule of the flesh. Nor had the authority of writing, of constitutions sanctified, in the best Nietzschean fashion, by blood, succeeded in effecting the disembodiment of power. The signs of racial and sexual subordination, read in bodies made textual, carried authority and power with them. In racial and sexual hierarchies, power was disseminated, democratized. All men, having eaten the flesh of the father, might share in his authority over women. Settlers, vested by law and scientific literatures with racial superiority, held the power disseminated in those signs. They held authority, as kings once had, in the flesh, and it was in that flesh that their authority would be challenged. The ritual deaths would be exacted and enacted again in the deaths of settlers and colonists who had similarly claimed the title to rule, not in their blood but in their skin.

The "morality" of decolonization with regard to the settler is simple, Frantz Fanon wrote in *The Wretched of the Earth:* the imperative is "to put him out of the picture." The native "has already decided to eject him and to take his place." This displacement and replacement of the settler was to be accomplished, like the revolutionary replacements that preceded it, through violence. Those who ruled in the body would find their authority disputed there. The assault on these intimate citadels of privilege would, like the regicides, like the Terror, undo more than particular bodies. As Fanon writes, "It is a whole material and moral universe that is breaking up."[4]

The violence of decolonization, like the violence of the Terror, has been often portrayed as a mistaken excess. The colonized, unable in their ignorance or rage to distinguish legitimate political targets, attacked all settlers randomly. The violence of anticolonial terror was not, however, as random as it seemed. The refusal to confine attacks to holders of political or military office recognized that the machinery of power and violence extended beyond the holders of office to the holders of a broader imperial status. As Albert Memmi observed, the colonizers, even those of goodwill, share a guilt consequent on the enjoyment of undeserved privilege. In his notorious introduction to Fanon's work, Jean-Paul Sartre (mindful, perhaps, of Saint Just's argument that no reign is innocent) endorsed the informal executions in the colonies. "Make no mistake about it," Sartre insists, "by this bitterness and spleen, by their

ever-present desire to kill us, by the permanent tensing of powerful muscles which are afraid to relax, they have become men."[5] Sartre regarded
anticolonial violence as redemptive not only for the colonized but for
the colonizer: "violence, like Achilles' lance, can heal the wounds it has
inflicted."[6]

"The naked truth of decolonization evokes for us the searing bul-
lets and bloodstained knives which emanate from it."[7] The truth of
decolonization, and its power to dismantle a moral universe, began in
a great refusal; "we only become what we are by the radical and deep-
seated refusal of that which others have made of us."[8] The colonial
order had employed violence to conquer and pacify the colonized, to ter-
rorize them and render them subject. Colonial violence stripped the colonized of their humanity, depriving them of the exercise of will, the right
of dominion, and the integrity of their bodies. The killing of the colonizer, Fanon argued, returned to the colonized the humanity that colonization had denied them. "The colonized man finds his freedom in and
through violence," Fanon wrote. Through violence "the 'thing' which
has been colonized becomes man."[9]

"At the level of individuals," Fanon writes, "violence is a cleansing
force. It frees the native from his inferiority complex and from his
despair and inaction; it makes him fearless and restores his self-respect."
Violence not only makes the colonized human, it makes them a nation.
Fanon writes, "The practice of violence binds them together as a
whole."[10] Following Freud, Fanon affirms that violence secures the
capacity for self-government. "Yesterday they were completely irre-
sponsible; today they mean to understand everything and make all deci-
sions."[11] They acquire the right to make promises.

Fanon's account turns on the recognition of responsibility. That the
killings are done on behalf of the state does not absolve the individuals
who commit them of responsibility. On the contrary, it is the assumption of responsibility, of guilt, that binds the nation together.

In the penultimate chapter of *The Wretched of the Earth*, "Colonial
War and Mental Disorders," Fanon recounts a series of cases that came
to his psychiatric practice. These cases seem at first to offer a caution-
ary coda to the approbation of revolutionary violence that Fanon offers
in the text proper.[12] Yet Fanon's moral tales of justice and responsibility resist this reassuring reading.

Case number one concerns an Algerian, a soldier in the Front de
Libération Nationale (FLN), who became impotent following the rape
of his wife. His impotence, we learn, is more than sexual. He was trou-

bled by sleeplessness and absence of mind, and his superiors, thinking him ill, sent him for a medical examination.

> He avoided political discussion and showed a marked lack of interest in everything having to do with the national struggle. He avoided listening to any news which had a bearing on the war of liberation.[13]

The revolutionary had learned that his wife had been questioned by the French, refused to reveal her knowledge of his whereabouts or those of his comrades in the FLN, and was, in the course of questioning, raped by the French.

> That wasn't a simple rape, for want of something better to do, or for sadistic reasons like those I've had occasion to see in the villages; it was the rape of an obstinate woman, who was ready to put up with anything rather than sell her husband. And the husband in question, *it was me.*[14]

Ethics, Kant taught, is found in the triangulation of the general and the particular. Kant instructs us to look for the general principle in particular acts, to accord personal conduct to a general standard. The recognition of that general standard was not, however, sufficient for Fanon's revolutionary. He had "seen peasants drying the tears of their wives after having seen them raped under their very eyes." He had, with his comrades, "intervened in such circumstances in order to explain matters to the civilians."[15] He knew, and he had explained to others, where one's duty lay in such general circumstances. He had accepted it. Yet he found that the presence of the signifier in the sign has consequences that are profound, intimate, and inevitable. He knew the public significance of the woman's act. What he had not expected was the recognition of an all too private debt: "the husband in question, *it was me.*"[16]

We have become accustomed to seeing the abstract in the particular, to recognizing the public and political force of nominally private places, private acts. Fanon's cases oblige us to recognize that the private haunts the public.

Case number five concerns a European police inspector. "The thing that kills me most," he tells Fanon, "is the torture. You don't know what that is, do you? Sometimes I torture people for ten hours at a stretch." He had come to Fanon because he was bothered by what he called "fits of madness." He had begun to beat his wife and children, and "as soon as someone goes against me I want to hit him. . . . I say to myself, 'If I had you for a few hours my fine fellow you wouldn't look so clever afterwards.' "[17] Such impulses, the inspector reported, were foreign to him. They had come upon him only "since the troubles."[18] For this man, this agent of the state, the modern distinctions between private and public, person and office, did not hold. The practices of the torturer's profession became the practices of his private life as well. He might leave the interrogation rooms of prison and police station, but he carried the practices proper to those spaces within him. He was haunted by his victims.

Case number three, a young soldier of the FLN, was haunted as well. He was visited each night by a woman, "bloodless, pale, and terribly thin," with an open wound in her stomach. Each night she came to him and insisted that he should give her back her spilled blood. The patient, Fanon reports, knew who she was well enough—"it was he who had killed her." She was the wife of "an active colonialist" who had already killed two Algerian civilians. The soldier, whose mother had been killed by a French soldier, watched as she was questioned. "When I looked at her," he told Fanon, "I thought of my mother." He stabbed her, she died, he was taken into custody. "After that," he told Fanon, "this woman started coming every night and asking for my blood. But my mother's blood—where's that?"[19]

Who but the son carries the mother's blood?

The soldier's account might be read, as Fanon recognized, as "an unconscious guilt complex following on the death of the mother." One might incline particularly to this reading, as the son had been the support of the family since his father's death some years earlier, and the mother had been killed after the son joined the Maquis.[20] Such a reading, however, too easily reduces a political act to a private revenge. The question "But my mother's blood—where's that?" is given several answers in the soldier's account, none complete, none satisfactory. The mother's blood is spilled. The wife of the colonialist carries the mother's blood. The soldier carries the mother's blood. Each night the woman who is and is not the mother reclaims her blood, only to return, pale, bloodless, and demanding, the next night. Like the demand for the proofs of love, the demand for the mother's blood cannot be satisfied.[21] The mother's death cannot be recompensed. The killing of the colonialist's wife supplies a French death by an Algerian hand for an Algerian one by a French hand. Yet "when I looked at that woman I thought of my mother."[22] It was "a manifold repetition of the same woman."[23] Having taken the French woman for the mother and given her the mother's death, the soldier finds that he has indeed taken her for the mother, and his blood is hers.

"What recourse has the son who has killed the mother?" In Irigaray's reading of the *Eumenides,* the sacrifice of another mother and the absence of harm to men returns the one who kills to the community. He is "pure, a good citizen. Fit for life in common with free men. Perhaps even a potential king."[24] The death of the mother, of the other that is one's own, is absolved by another death, and a rational explanation. Guilt vanishes before the demands of politics and power.

Fanon's reading is more complex. The economy of exchange that exacted the French woman's death established an equivalence between French and Algerian, and in doing so made the Algerian soldier his own enemy. The assumption of the power and authority entailed passion and subjection. The son establishes a semiotic economy in which one woman may stand for another. In this economy, the colonizer becomes the equivalent of the colonized, the French woman's death answers for the death of the Algerian mother. The power of final judgment—claimed by the colonized as it was once claimed by the colonizer—is inevitably defeated by the economy of exchange on which revenge depends. With this, sexual divisions fall as well. The economy of exchange that makes it possible for the French woman's death to serve as payment for the death of the Algerian mother makes the son the murderer of his mother. Authority entails the assumption of blood guilt. Fanon reminds us: Those who are sacrificed, will be our own.

The most profound of the cases Fanon discusses is "a borderline case" that serves as a prologue to "Colonial War and Mental Disorders." Here Fanon writes of "a patriot who had been in the resistance" in one of the newly independent African countries. He had found himself suffering from insomnia, anxiety, and suicidal obsessions at the same time each year. "The critical date was that when on instructions from his organization he had placed a bomb somewhere. Ten people had been killed as a result." In the period immediately after the event, the revolutionary had not been troubled by these symptoms. They emerged when, after independence had been achieved, he encountered some former colonists and found he liked them. The revolutionary had, he observes, "never for a single moment thought of repudiating his past action." Fanon does not encourage him to do so. What interests Fanon, and should interest us, is that the revolutionary "realized very clearly the manner in which he himself had to pay the price of national independence. "In other words," Fanon writes,

> we are forever pursued by our actions. Their ordering, their circumstances, and their motivation may perfectly well come to be profoundly modified a posteriori. This is merely one of the snares that history and its various influences sets for us. But can we escape becoming dizzy? And who can affirm that vertigo does not haunt the whole of existence?[25]

In Fanon's account, action on behalf of the sovereign offers no absolution. The individual who kills for the revolution takes the responsibility for those deaths. What does it mean to take a death upon oneself?

For Abraham, as for the revolutionaries, innocent death is the price of political power. "I have made you the father of a multitude of nations" God says to Abraham.

> I will make you exceedingly fruitful; and I will make nations of you, and kings shall come forth from you. And I will establish my covenant between me and you and your descendants.[26]

Abraham's right to make promises follows his willingness to offer up an innocent death. For Derrida, "it is as if Abraham had *already* killed Isaac" in the instant in which he raised his hand.[27] God, in Derrida's account, takes the intention for the act. Abraham has understood and acted upon his duty to God. He has assumed absolute responsibility. He is willing to kill; he "had the courage to behave like a murderer in the eyes of the world . . . in the eyes of morality and politics."[28]

Derrida recognizes the story of Abraham as one that is reproduced, reenacted, endlessly in the quotidian. "Day and night, at every instant, on all the Mount Moriahs of this world, I am doing that, raising my knife over what I love and must love, over those to whom I owe absolute fidelity, incommensurably." Each commitment to another entails the neglect, the refusal, of an obligation to all others.[29] Absolute duty, each duty, involves the sacrifice of others.

For Abraham, Derrida writes, this "absolute duty" entails no burden of guilt or regret.

> Without being so, then, he nevertheless feels absolved of his duty towards his family, towards the human species [le genre humaine] and the generality of the ethical, absolved by the absolute of a unique duty that binds him to God the one.[30]

Derrida's account has the divinity demanding the proofs of love.

> The command requests, like a prayer from God, a declaration of love that implores: tell me that you love me, that you turn towards me, towards the unique one, towards the other as unique and, above all, over everything else, unconditionally, and in order to do that, make a gift of death, give death to your only son and give me the death I ask for.[31]

The demand for the proofs of love is the demand that cannot be finally satisfied, that renews itself inevitably in the moment of its satisfaction. Yet God's demand does not renew itself. Isaac is not sacrificed. Abraham's covenant with God is sealed not by bloodshed but by the evasion of bloodshed. This is the contract that does not depend on fulfillment for its authority.

Politics offers no such evasion, no saving diversion. Fanon's cases bear witness instead to the impossibility of absolution. Those who assume responsibility in Fanon—as in Freud and Nietzsche—assume the burden of guilt with it. Fanon's work obliges us to recognize that those who kill, whether they do so on their own behalf or on behalf of the nation, as a refusal of injustice or in pursuit of justice, with their own hands or through the state, will nevertheless remain (whether they wish to be or not) responsible for their actions. The assumption of this responsibility enables the once-animal to make themselves human, and citizens. They acquire the right to make promises, they become self-governing, they band together, they restore their lost humanity.

The recognition of the power of one person to kill another contains within it a comprehensive claim: the power of the will, the desire to extend that will in the world, the claim that one might have—in the final sense—dominion over others. This power is common to all, marking an equality founded not only in subjection but in a common capacity for dominion.

The killing of colonists and kings ended regimes. These deaths cast not only monarchs but monarchy, not only colonists but colonialism, into oblivion. They seem to give us closure, to remove us from the power of claims to power in the blood, from the rule of men to the rule of law. Yet one need not believe in an afterlife to find oneself haunted in this one. We are left with the specters Nietzsche raised when he declared that violence is necessary to give an animal the right to make promises. We are left with Freud's myth in which the ghosts of the father speak in the sons who swallowed him. We are left with the haunting memory of Fanon's revolutionary, who believed that he had killed the innocent and would not disavow it.

If we are to be haunted, let the ghosts be great ones. But if we find that what we chose to cast into oblivion returns to make its home in us, what then?

# 14
## The Fire Next Time

Race revealed (as it enacted) a semiotic economy that made word and flesh, race and revolution, revolutionary France and revolutionary Africa interchangeable. The fire of Prometheus could stand for the fire next time, the revolutionary past for the revolution yet to come. Race permitted such exchanges of space for space, time for time, through the mediating exchange of word for flesh, and flesh for word. The problematics of race were written on the bodies of untimely revolutionaries.

Carlyle's French Revolution had both race and sex. The image of fire that made France Semele and burned the revolution black. The revolution, Carlyle wrote, was "a Blackness naturally of Erebus." The revolutionaries were blackened as well. Carlyle's account writes race on the revolutionaries, making them people of color in skin or sympathy. Theroigne was a "brown, eloquent Beauty," Danton a "huge, brawny figure" with "black brows, and rude, flattened face."[1] Brissot was "the friend of Blacks," Marat a "swart bird." Mirabeau too was "swart burly-headed Mirabeau" with "thick black locks" and a "black boar's head." In the ranks were "Brissot, the friend of Blacks," "D'Espremenil, with his tropical heat (he was born in Madras); with his dusky, confused violence," "dusky D'Espremenil," "Dame de Fontenai, brown beautiful woman," and "that other olive-complexioned individual, the artillery officer in Toulon." The "individual" is Napoleon, whom Carlyle elsewhere calls "that little bronze-complexioned Artillery-Officer." He appears as more creole than Josephine, as the amalgam of "Black Sansculottism" and "White Patriotism."[2]

The France of the revolution had become the abode of Tigers and Cannibals, the dark continent of Carlyle's imaginary.[3] The revolutionaries were animals and heathens. There Mirabeau walks and "shakes his black chevelure, or lion's mane." He was the "roughest lion's whelp ever littered out of that rough breed." "How the old lion (for our old Marquis too was lionlike, most unconquerable, kingly-genial, and most perverse) gazed wondering upon his off-spring and determined to train him as no lion had yet been!"[4] In this dark continent "reverberates the lion-voice of Danton." Danton will defy his enemies "with the roar of a lion in the toils."[5] Some go more quietly, but no less dangerously. "Does not a feline Maximilien stalk there . . . back bent and hair up?"[6] Carlyle echoed the reports of the revolution to an earlier England.

Romilly had likened revolutionary France to "a republic of tigers in some forest in Africa." Wordsworth saw revolutionary Paris as "a wood where tigers roam." The sans-culottes, Wollstonecraft had written, were "barbarous beyond the tiger's cruelty." She concurred with Burke, who had declared the Jacobins more rapacious than "wolves and tigers." The *Times* saw the tiger in Marat. "His eyes resembled those of the tyger cat, and there was a kind of ferociousness in his looks that corresponded with the savage fierceness of that animal." An anti-Jacobin pamphlet of the day declared the "tyrannicide mob" of Paris a "tygerish multitude." If the French had once been, in a phrase of Voltaire's (echoed by John Wilkes), "a nation of monkeys and tigers," "the fact is that the Monkey-compound has disappeared with the Aristocratical part of the Community, and has left the wanton cruelty of the Tyger to be claimed exclusively by the Democracy."[7]

They were close to the beasts and the gods, these revolutionary inhabitants of an all-too-alien, all-too-African France. Carlyle locates them in the wilderness and inscribes upon each revolutionary name the signs of the other and the alien. Robespierre becomes "Mahomet Robespierre." He is the prophet of "a conscious Mumbo-Jumbo" beside which the "Mumbo-Jumbo of the African woods to me seems venerable." "Mumbo is Mumbo and Robespierre is his Prophet." Carlyle's Robespierre is preeminently the False Prophet, and Carlyle gives him to us dressed in the colors of all false prophets, Muslim, African, Asian, and Catholic. He is "Chief Priest," "Trismegistus and Dalai-Lama." Robespierre is the "seagreen Pontiff" worshiped by devout women, with "Jacobins kissing the hem of his garment." He pleads with "jesuitical dexterity," his speech "as smooth as a Jesuit Doctor's." Robespierre is guillotined, the false prophet is overthrown only to be replaced by the

"Orphic witchery" and "dancing Houris of a Mahomet's paradise, much too Mahometan." For Carlyle, one heathenism is much the same as another, though he might in a pinch prefer the innocent African Mumbo to the canting, "*conscious* Mumbo-Jumbo" of the French disciples of "Fifth Evangelist Jean-Jacques."[8]

In this metaphoric cosmos it is Robespierre, high priest of a secular divinity, who is marked as most thoroughly alien. He is the color of no human being, this "seagreen ghost," this "seagreen Chimera." Robespierre was "not a man with the heart of a man, but a poor spasmodic incorruptible pedant, with a logic-formula instead of a heart." The warm familial affections Carlyle details for each of the black revolutionaries are absent here. Though he methodically notes Augustin's willingness to share his brother's death, he erases the presence, intimacy, and influence of Charlotte. Carlyle's Robespierre is a man without women, singular and celibate as the icons of Richelieu. Robespierre stands apart in his coldness, his cruelty, his sartorial fastidiousness. "The Incorruptible himself sits apart; or is seen stalking in solitary places," he "held himself apart." He "has his being solely in formulas."[9]

In Burke's French Revolution, abstractions and formulas belong to the Jew, or rather to "Jew and Jacobin." Carlyle deployed the figure of the Jew differently. This is a role to which the Jacobin cannot pretend. He asks sardonically, "*This* is the miraculous Aaron's Rod thou wilt stretch over a hag-ridden, hell-ridden France, and bid her plagues cease?" The "Jacobin sounding-board" might proclaim, "To your tents, O Israel!" but Jacobins are not Jews in Carlyle's account. "No symbolic Ark, like the old Hebrews, do these men bear" though they too have a covenant.[10] For Carlyle as for Burke, Jews are the people of scripture. For Carlyle, however, they are still the chosen people, and their name belongs not to the heathenish, philosophic followers of Jean-Jacques Evangel but to the Puritans, English and American. In the court of a not-yet-revolutionary France, the American plenipotentiaries, Deane and Franklin stand as "the sons of the Saxon Puritans, with their Old-Saxon temper, Old-Hebrew culture . . . among the light children of Heathenism, Monarchy, Sentimentalism, and the Scarlet Woman."[11] These "Saxon Hebrews" are revolutionaries after Cromwell.

All the language, all the forms, of otherness serve Carlyle, but they are not conflated. Blackness marks the primitive and the innocent, those burning with the fire of revolution, those who will be consumed in it. They are ascribed an animal vigor, a heroic physicality. Carlyle entitles one chapter "Danton, no weakness" and praises Danton as "monstrous colossal Reality," "Titan of the Revolution."[12] Danton is, like the Titans, earth-born, from "good farmer-people" and "from the great fire-bosom of Nature herself."[13] Mirabeau too is "Titanic," "the giant Mirabeau," "Heathen and Titan," who, "like a burning mountain blazes heaven-high."[14] Theroigne, the "Brown, eloquent beauty," is "fire-hearted."[15] Blackness is the color of earth and fire, the colour of the materials that are fire's source and of those touched by fire. With this amalgam of earth and fire, Carlyle places black revolutionaries in the realm of myth. They are Promethean: earth-born, primitive, but bringing fire to men. The fire would consume them.

The ancient race of the Titans was, however, not the nearest referent for blackness. Carlyle's account draws upon the more mundane meanings assigned to blackness as a mark of racial difference. The black race of the revolution is primitive and heathen, with earthy appetites. Mirabeau is a "Love-hero, with the strength of thirty men"; he has "all manner of women." The Amazon Theroigne is "light-behaved." The "brown, beautiful woman" seduces. Carlyle himself is seduced by the "dingy" Camille Desmoulins; "it were but falsehood to pretend one did not almost love thee, thou headlong, lightly sparkling man."[16] Even swart Marat is coupled with his washerwoman. The primitive sensuality that conventional racism read in blackness is written into the blackness assigned these revolutionaries. They belong to a world not only of natural rights, but of natural lusts and natural satisfactions; of unrestrained, unregulated desires. For Carlyle the erotic and the political were confounded in the heat of desire.

In Carlyle's account, as in Carlyle's historical Britain, blackness was the color of desire. Blackness marked the desired body of the colonized. The colonial enterprises that sent Carlyle's imperial compatriots into Africa and Asia marked blackness as the color of desire: the desire for land and dominion, the desire for wealth, the desire for all the pleasures and satisfactions, sensual and spiritual, that remained foreign to the metropole. The resistance of the Zulus and the Somalis, of the Mutiny, of Tipu Sultan and the Rani of Jhansi made blackness the color of the desire for freedom.

Here too, blackness was the color of fire. Carlyle gives the Black Jacobins short shrift in this account. Yet we hear "of Brissot and his *Friends of the Blacks*" and, with them, "of a whole St. Domingo blazing skyward; blazing in literal fire, and in far worse metaphorical, beaconing the nightly main." The Plain of Cap Français became a "variegated Glitter and nocturnal Fulgor . . . one huge whirl of smoke and flame."

These were, as Carlyle makes clear in the passage that follows, fires of "Levelling," fires of amalgamation. He quotes the demonstration of the insurrectionist "Quarteroon Oge": "He took black powder or seedgrains in the hollow of his hand, this Oge, sprinkled a film of white ones on the top, and said to his Judges, 'Behold, they are white'; then *shook* his hand, and said, 'Where are the whites, *où sont les blancs?*' "[17] What was in the hand of this revolutionary? Gunpowder or seedgrains? Fertility or destruction? St. Domingo becomes, "as African Haiti, a monition to the world."[18] Whom does it admonish? The evocative gesture of the prophet Oge becomes for Carlyle a warning not only to Haiti but to France, not only to France but to England. The disappearance of the white among the black, the threatened amalgamation of goods and people in the fires of revolution, forecast a struggle not only for liberty but for equality.

Black was the color of liberty; black was the color of equality. The warring signs of blackness and whiteness referred to class as well as race. Carlyle writes that wigs were made of the hair of guillotined women. "The locks of a Duchess may come to cover the scalp of a Cordwainer; her blonde German Frankism his black Gaelic poll."[19] There is an old connection, as Baudrillard reminds us, between counterfeiting and democracy. Counterfeiting belongs to "the destructuring of the feudal order by the bourgeois order, and the emergence of open competition"; it marks the emergence of "competitive democracy."[20] The revolutionary recognition that the signs of rank are detachable is given a material enactment in Carlyle's anecdote. The racial differences assigned to Frank and Gael, to swart Marat and the "fair," "king-descended, god-descended" Princesse de Lamballe were coincident with class.[21] The Gaelic laborer in Britain or in France might learn to cover the signs of subordination with the signifiers of a higher status, counterfeiting a rank that blood would not permit him to pretend to.

For Blake, as for Carlyle, the signs of rank were detachable, exchangeable. Carlyle was suspicious of the instability, the dynamism, the incessant movement of revolution. Blake saw flight as an attribute of joy and life. For Blake, as for Burke, the signs of rank might be stripped away. Both saw truth in this nakedness, but Burke (like Nietzsche) saw modesty outraged by the revelation. Blake could stand naked in the presence of nakedness, unashamed.

The defeat of Mystery would bring down kings and councilors, great men and warriors. "Who shall mourn for Mystery," Blake asks, "who never loosed her captives?"

> Let the slave grinding at the mill run out into the field;
> Let him look up into the heavens and laugh in the bright air;
> Let the enchained soul, shut up in darkness and in sighing
> Whose face has never seen a smile in thirty weary years,
> Rise and look out, his chains and dungeon door are open.
> And let his wife and children return from the oppressor's scourge.
> They look behind at every step and believe it is a dream.

The Jubilee Blake prophesies joins "all the slaves from every earth in the wide universe": millworker and peasant, prisoners and slaves, male and female, black and white. He gives their song of celebration to "an African black."[22]

Blake expected that truth would strip away not only the inscriptions of rank but those of race as well. For Blake, "these black bodies and this sunburnt face, is but a cloud" protecting human beings from the heat of divine love. "When our souls have learnt the heat to bear, the cloud will vanish" for black and white alike. Blake's "little black boy" looks forward to unity with the English boy, when they, "I from black and he from white cloud free," find themselves in the presence of God.[23]

Blake suggests, however, that the black child is, in his blackness, closer to God. The black child can stand unveiled in the presence of God, but the English child must be shielded from the strength of divine love.

> I'll shade him from the heat till he can bear
> To lean in joy upon our father's knee.

God lives in the rising sun, "and gives his light and gives his heat away."

> And we are put on earth a little space
> That we may learn to bear the beams of love.[24]

The black child, sheltering the white, can bear those beams more readily. Blackness is not merely an artifact of climate. Blackness belongs to those already touched by fire.

"Fiery Orc," the revolutionary spirit who awakens and enflames America, is "the image of God who dwells in the darkness of Africa."[25] The revolutionary Americans are "indignant, burning with the fires of Orc." Burke had argued in "Speech on Conciliation with the Colonies" that Americans derived their love of freedom from their dominion over their black slaves. Blake, like Aeschylus, saw the passion for freedom in the form of the oppressed. When he came to draw Orc, the animating spirit of American revolution, he gave him the form of a rebellious slave.

Blake had been commissioned to engrave plates to illustrate J. G. Stedman's *Narrative of a Five Years' Expedition Against the Revolted Negroes of Surinam.* His engravings, David Erdman wrote, "emphasize the dignity of Negro men and women stoical under cruel torture." One of the engravings, "the image of the courageous rebel on the cruciform rack bit into his heart," and in the Preludium of "America" he drew Orc in the same posture to represent the spirit of human freedom defiant of tyranny.[26]

In the American Revolution, in the revolutions in France and England, in Asia and Africa, in Santo Domingo,

> Raging furious, the flames of desire
> Ran through heaven and earth, living flames,
> Intelligent, organized, armed
> With destruction and plagues.[27]

These revolutionaries are possessed, like Burke's, by the furies of hell. They are demonic, they are lost to shame. They rage, and their rage is "intelligent, organized, armed." They are not only the liberators of the Bastille, inflamed by a hot, immediate passion. They are the authors of the Terror, fired with the "living flames of intellect." Those flames leap oceans to fire continents. Dr. Richard Price's sermon concludes with a peroration that is at once a prophecy and a call to arms.

> Behold, the light you have struck out, after setting AMERICA free, reflected to FRANCE, and there kindled into a blaze that lays despotism in ashes, and warms and illuminates EUROPE![28]

Blake's preface to "Jerusalem" addresses a reader for whom intellect and desire, reason and revelation are conjoined. Blake's god leaps time as well as continents, alien neither to paganism nor the Enlightenment. This is "that God from whom all books are given,"

> Who in mysterious Sinai's awful cave
> To man the wondrous art of writing gave.
> Again he speaks in thunder and in fire—
> Thunder of thought and flames of fierce desire.[29]

This God, like the demon Orc, is Promethean. The divine, pentecostal fire descends not to the priests but to the people. The Third Estate "convene in the Hall of Nations; like spirits of fire in the beautiful porches of the sun."[30] The revolutionary walks through fire; "his feet become like brass, his knees and thighs like silver, and his breast and head like gold."[31]

The aporias of revolution become incarnate in the inconstant, iridescent forms of the revolutionaries. They are born, like the race of the Titans, from earth and fire, "in furrows rent by the lightnings of the Enlightenment."[32] They are black, they are red, they are white; they are demons, they are human, they are tigers. They are lions who ask, "How is it we have walked through fire and yet are not consumed?"[33] They are men who walk through fire and take on a shimmering, metallic form. They are constantly changing, and yet it is not change that they incarnate. They are on their way to something.

They move forward into uncharted territory, uncertain terrain. "Tell me what is a thought, and of what substance is it made? . . . Tell me where dwell the thoughts forgotten till thou call them forth?" Blake asks, and then, "Are there other wars beside the wars of sword and fire? And are there other sorrows besides the sorrows of poverty?" "Who taught thee modesty?" he asks, and "With what sense does the parson claim the labour of the farmer?"[34] Blake is replete with "strange, wicked, questionable questions." The questions Blake asks of the tiger are questions for a revolution.

> What immortal hand or eye
> Could frame thy fearful symmetry?
>
> In what distant deeps or skies
> Burnt the fire of thine eyes?
> On what wings dare he aspire?
> What the hand dare seize the fire?
>
> And what shoulder and what art
> Could twist the sinews of thy heart?
> And when thy heart began to beat,
> What dread hand? And what dread feet?
>
> What the hammer? What the chain?
> In what furnace was thy brain?
> What the anvil? What dread grasp
> Dare its deadly terrors clasp?

The work of revolution is not only a work of ecstatic liberation, it is a work of terror. The revolutionaries are "intelligent, organized, armed with plagues and destruction." "How," Nietzsche asked, "can one create a memory for the human animal?" He answered that man "could never do without blood, torture, and sacrifices when he felt the need to create a memory for himself."[35] Forgetfulness may be more difficult than memory. What is to erase a long training in subjection? What will remove unconscious habits of deference? What will overcome an acquired taste for abjection? In France, it was to be bloodshed.

> When the stars threw down their spears
> And watered heaven with their tears,
> Did he smile his work to see?
> Did he who made the Lamb make thee?[36]

Burke and Carlyle wept with the celestials. Paine and Price (how apt their names are here) are ranged with the demiurge. Wollstonecraft too could name the hardships of poverty and abjection, the dearths and deaths, the assaults and the many forms of humiliation that the aristocracy required of the people. She could ask, "What were the outrages of a day to these continual miseries?" Though she judged the bloodshed of the "tygerish multitude" excessive, she nevertheless recognized that "such misery demands more than tears."[37] It demands divine judgment.

Blake was not the first to recognize the work of revolution as divine. The hands that author revolutions make themselves immortal. "It would take gods to give men laws," Rousseau wrote. The divinity of democratic revolutions lies not only in their capacity to create but in their capacity to destroy. These revolutions cast much into the fire, they cast all in question. They seed time and the nations with a fertile abandon. Yet their beauty lies not only in their generous disorderliness but in the ruling proportion that underwrites them. They are made beautiful and divine in their fearful symmetry. These revolutions are the work of an immortal eye.

Tocqueville ends *Democracy in America,* a book written on one revolution for another, with a remembrance of what was lost in aristocracy.

> When I survey this countless multitude of beings, shaped in each
> other's likeness, among whom nothing stands out or falls unduly low,
> the sight of such universal uniformity saddens and chills me, and I am
> tempted to regret that state of society which has ceased to be.

This, Tocqueville instructs himself, is the view of man, who can turn from one thing to contemplate another. Tocqueville could not readily see difference in equality, the variety of tastes and desires, ambitions and abilities, present in a "countless multitude" of equals. Yet if he could not see, he nevertheless knew that the sight of the divine might differ from his own. If he could not see beauty in equality, he nevertheless knew that there were forms of beauty greater than his apprehensions. God, the author who sees all things and yet remains unseen, should, Tocqueville tells himself, be pleased with equality.

> It is natural to suppose that not the particular prosperity of the few, but the greater well-being of all is most pleasing in the sight of the Creator and Preserver of men. What seems to me decay is thus in his eyes progress; what pains me is acceptable to him. Equality may be less elevated, but it is more just, and in its justice lies its greatness and beauty.[38]

In my time, we remain far from that justice. Those revolutionaries, with "their laps full of seed, their hands full of generous fire," brought into being not only our nations but the nations we have not yet achieved.[39] The fires they set are burned to embers now, but we still warm our hands and fire our hearts by them.

# 15

## Semele, or the Enlightenment in Flames

"France had looked upon Democracy; seen it face to face."[1] When God spoke to Moses from within the burning bush, flame served as the veil of the deity. France was to have a more intimate communication. France was Semele. France was the Enlightenment in flames.

In this vision, shared by Carlyle and Cixous, Blake and Irigaray, the woman's body is the site of the revolutionary aporia. Open and empty, boundaries torn apart, this body was the sight of fertility and destruction. On this site, the old certainties burst into flame and were burned to ashes.

Revolutionary France was black for Blake and Carlyle, feminine for Carlyle and Burke: the woman armed. Burke, Carlyle, and Blake all read it as Promethean: titanic, earthy, enlightening, inflammatory. They and their contemporaries saw the revolution as a woman at once barren and fecund, her "lap full of dangerous fire." Some saw themselves as born—forged—in that fire.

Carlyle's is a vision of the Enlightenment open and impassioned, a vision of revolutionary lack and desire, a vision of the spirits and monsters that this Enlightenment, black and feminine, African and animal, would bring forth. Carlyle sees the republican Semele, quickened by the Enlightenment, full of fire. What does she bear: Dionysos, a cry, an emptiness, or the divine?

The streets of Paris became a "womb" containing those "monsters and prodigies of Events, which thou seest her visibly bear." Yet, Carlyle declares, History cannot discover "what the secrets of its dark womb were." It is "a Blackness naturally of Erebus," yet "the lightening it held did in confused brightness strike forth." The dark womb had borne "monsters and prodigies of Events," but when the Jacobins fell, "childless, most decrepit, as we saw, sat the mighty Mother."[2]

The revolution was a tigress. The women of the revolution were dark women, barren women, women in flames. "But where is the brown-locked, light-behaved, fire-hearted Demoiselle Theroigne?" A pike and a straitjacket waited for her, Carlyle writes; "Better hadst thou stayed in thy native Luxembourg, and been the mother of some brave man's children."[3] For Carlyle, as for Burke, the French Revolution was at its heart, or, more precisely, had as its womb the insurrection of women. The men of the revolution were feminine as well. L'Amourette becomes a "Delilah-doxy"; the deputies exchange the "Delilah kiss."[4] Marat is "Cassandra-Marat" calling up troops armed "with dirk and muff."[5] This is the revolution of Delilah, of Jezebel, of Medusa, who would, "with her snaky-sparkling head, illuminate this murk."[6]

Carlyle saw revolutionary passion abandon the rational individual, abandon Burke's "manly, moral, and regulated liberty." Carlyle's canny man was the "Single Person," the "King, Konning, Canning or Supremely Able-Man," the knowing one, the rational individual.[7] The republic was the uncanny place, the womb and the grave, the site of "Sansculottism consummating itself," the dangerous zone of the black and feminine, of an iridescent sexuality and an aporetic will.[8]

> Republic One and Indivisible! She is the newest Birth of Nature's waste inorganic Deep, which men name Orcus, Chaos, primeval Night; and knows one law, that of self-preservation. Tigresse Nationale: meddle not with a whisker of her.[9]

This Mother Society, this Orcus with the "gloomy womb," has "a preternatural life in her."[10] She is barren, but she brings forth the republic. Her womb is dark, her womb is full of light. She might have been better described by Nietzsche's answered riddle.

> Light is all that I conceive
> Ashes everything I leave.
> Flame I am, assuredly.[11]

The flames that burned out sham, the clarity that challenged unjust empires, had touched heaven. Carlyle saw heaven burst into flame at the touch and become "as red as Hellfire." The boundaries between heaven and hell were fragile indeed. Carlyle saw the revolutionaries— the revolution—go beyond good and evil. The French had become a nation "full of wants and devoid of habits."[12] They had become a people who were not longer what they had been and who were not yet what they would become. They were a people full of appetite and desire.

For Burke, as for Carlyle, the vision of the revolution as feminine captured its violent indeterminacy. The revolution was

> a vast, tremendous, unformed spectre, in a far more terrific guise than any which ever yet have overpowered the imagination, and subdued the fortitude of man. Going straight forward to its end, unappalled by peril, unchecked by remorse, despising all common maxims and all common means, that hideous phantom overpowered those who could not believe it was possible she could at all exist.[13]

She was beyond convention, beyond good and evil, beyond the reason and the imaginations of men. She was being and nonbeing, destruction and fertility. What would come of her?

When Burke and Carlyle looked into the revolution they saw the woman in flames, an empty womb filled with fire and a void, an Enlightenment burned to ashes. There is also, in the image of Semele, the possibility of an improbable conception in the ashes.

Did the revolution give off light? Certainly, Carlyle thought, it was inflamed. "Shams are burnt up . . . the very Cant of them is burnt up."

> Does the EMPIRE OF IMPOSTURE waver? Burst there in starry sheen up-darting, Light-rays from out of its dark foundations; as it rocks and heaves, not in travail-throes but in death throes? Yea, light-rays, piercing, clear, that salute the heavens -lo they kindle it; their starry clearness becomes as red Hellfire.[14]

The fire of the Enlightenment had burned out the pretenses of feudalism, and something had quickened in the destruction.

She grew slowly in the ashes of revolution, but she was "her own sister-daughter," "herself giver as her mother and child."[15] She was "volcanic," "an explosive, utterly destructive, staggering return, with a force never yet unleashed and equal to the most forbidding of suppressions."[16] Cixous named her the Medusa and wrote, "You have only to look at the Medusa straight on to see her. And she's not deadly. She's beautiful and she's laughing."[17]

For Cixous, as for Carlyle and Blake, black was the color of those touched by fire. "We are black and we are beautiful," Cixous writes, and, echoing Blake, "Because you are Africa, you are black. Your continent is dark."[18] This is the territory of revolution, the place of the fire next time. This had been the place of those who cannot represent themselves but must be represented, who found themselves ruled in the word and the flesh. "Woman must write her self: must write about women and bring women to writing," Cixous writes. Writing is that which has been denied to women: to write, to be written, to write themselves, to write themselves writing. And, as with the colonized, writing is that which remade the body as alien territory, a place of exile, imprisonment, and subjection. "By writing herself, woman will return to the body which has been more than confiscated from her, which has been turned into the uncanny stranger on display."[19] Women were driven away violently from writing and from their bodies, "for the same reasons, by the same law."[20]

Cixous's Medusa exhorts, "Writing is for you, you are for you, your body is yours, take it."[21] Writing, the pursuit of the drive to writing, would make the body heard. "Write your self. Your body must be heard." Hearing would make the woman's word visible, for those who listen to women speak see them inscribe their words on their bodies. She "physically materializes what she's thinking, she signifies it with her body . . . she inscribes what she's saying."[22] The word and the flesh, logic and passion, speech and writing, and all the senses are confounded in her. Her writing is heard, those who listen see.

This is Medusa, this is Semele, this is the Enlightenment in flames. Cixous writes, "Nearly the entire history of writing is confounded with the history of reason, of which it is at once the effect, the support, and one of the privileged alibis."[23] Through writing Semele would "forge for herself the antilogos weapon." Cixous has the modern's faith in writing; for her, "writing is precisely *the very possibility of change,* the space that can serve as a springboard for subversive thought, the precursory movement of a transformation of social and cultural structures," but her modernity is "the epoch that lives for the future, that opens itself up to the novelty of the future."[24] Writing undoes itself in Cixous: the written is heard as well as seen, the text becomes "precursory." No longer coupled with the logos, writing becomes "the antilogos weapon," the practice that escapes definition, "that can never be theorized, enclosed, coded."[25] The traditional medium of history becomes history's undoing, as those subjected to history, in history, by history, right themselves. "As subject for history, woman always occurs simultaneously in several places. Woman unthinks the unifying, regulating history that homogenizes and channels forces, herding contradictions onto a single battlefield."[26] History reveals itself to women, as it did to Fanon, as vertigo.

# Section 5

# 16
## The Laughter of Demeter

We reside in Weber's disenchanted world, a world of law and letters, yet we see bloodrites and sacrifice, origin myths and political phantasms. Weber and Barthes, Blumenberg and Wolin argue that myth is dead, yet we see the revival of myths and mythic form in Nietzsche, Freud, Derrida, Lacan, Irigaray. They offer commentaries on ancient myths; they compose new ones. They accept myth, those untimely ones, as a form in which political philosophy can be couched, give pleasure, and be made productive.

Enlightenment philosophy argued for the suppression of myth. Myth was said to compel belief without reason, and in the lexicon of the Enlightenment it became a synonym for falsehood. Reason is veiled in myth, concealed by an unaccustomed modesty. Reason works in myth unconscious of its own validating procedures. Those who recognize the work of language on the mind, the presence of order and meaning in the unconscious, in that which is not yet said, not yet sayable, turn easily to myth. The reason in myth—the reason for it, and the reason of it—are already visible to them. The veil attracts the gaze it denies.

Nietzsche sees in the myth of Baubo a site where the meaning of woman and of truth are conjoined. "Perhaps Truth is a woman who has reasons for not letting us see her reasons. Perhaps her name is—to speak Greek—Baubo."[1] In Nietzsche's telling, the unveilings of the Enlightenment appear as intrusions and violations, impelled by ignorance of what we know lies beneath the veil. The myth of the woman's genitals as empty and productive, barren and fertile, with reason and against it, serves Nietzsche as a fable for his—and our—relation to language: "We are all philologists now."

Behind, before, Nietzsche's writing are Jerusalem and Athens, the mythic languages of Greeks, Christians, and Jews. The laughter of Sarah echoes the laughter of Demeter; the advent of Iakchos prefigures the advent of Christ. For Greeks, Christians, and Jews, Nietzsche sees, something stands behind and before the word.

The myth in which Baubo appears begins with the fasting and infertility of Demeter. She is not filled and she does not bring forth. As she wanders the barren earth, she comes to a house. This is the place of Baubo, whose name means "belly"; this is the place of Dysaules, whose name means "house where it is not good to dwell."[2] This is the *unheimlich* place that is our first home: the womb. Demeter enters the house, and Baubo offers her a drink. She refuses it. Baubo then raises her skirts, revealing herself—her sex, her (as one commentator has it) "uncomely womb"—to Demeter.[3] Demeter laughs, and with this utterance her fertility returns.[4]

This is a mythic image that, in an age when we are told that myth is dead, nevertheless retains its mythic power: to enlighten, to reveal, to shock, to frighten, to amuse—to suggest, as Nietzsche suggested, a truth beyond what we commonly count as reason. Baubo is an image of the fertility of woman, the site of our origins. She is the empty place in women which is fertile and productive, a personification of the vagina and the womb. She is the site and sight of women's sexuality: the earthy place, the visible lack, the place of a monstrous—fearful and wonderful—apprehension. She reveals herself as the place of linguistic origin. Baubo's are the "lips that never did speak." She is the silent mouth, the empty place from which language comes.

In the myth, the sight of Baubo brings pleasure, laughter, fertility, and power to women. Freud would tell the myth differently. In Freud's stories, the sight of Baubo is given not to a grown woman but to male children.

> If, afterwards, a boy makes the discovery of the vagina from seeing his little sister or a girl playmate, he tries, to begin with, to disavow the evidence of his senses, for he cannot imagine a human being without such a precious portion. Later on, he takes fright at the possibility thus presented to him; and any threats that might have been made to him earlier because he took too great an interest in his little organ, now produce a deferred effect. He comes under the sway of the castration complex.[5]

The sight brings not laughter but terror, not fertility but impotence, not the return of an accustomed power but an unprecedented fear. The image showed Demeter what she had had; it showed Freud's child what he might come to lack. Freud's child confronted what was once one's own and revealed in its place an alien other, maimed and defective, whose loss of power carried within it a threat to oneself. Demeter confronted the other who is one's own, another self, or a familiar other, whose revealed power promised the return of one's own.

Freud was not alone in seeing Baubo as Medusa. An illustration of Charles Eisen to a fable of La Fontaine shows the devil frightened by the raised skirt of a young woman.[6] For Eisen and La Fontaine, as for Freud, to look at the feminine was to look on lack, upon the Medusa: a sight that turns mortal and immortal men to stone. The sight of the Medusa's hair of snakes, her face, her mouth, is the site of castration. It deprives men of power. But this is also Courbet's "origin of the world": the sight of generation.

For Nietzsche, fear and revelation are conjoined in the sight of Baubo, in the apprehension of the "strange, wicked, questionable character" of the will to truth.[7] Nietzsche's version of the myth leaves his relation to Baubo in question. If he did not, like the shameless Egyptian youths, lift the veil, did she, for her part, lift her skirt for him?

In the image of Baubo woman is constructed as the place where sexuality and speech, blood and language, meet. She is the locus of production: the empty womb, the silent mouth. In order to see this more clearly, we must return to myth, to the story of Demeter in the Eleusinian Mysteries. We must see something of what Demeter saw in the moment of Baubo's revelation. "It would not be easy," Kerenyi acknowledges, "to describe more exactly what it was that Demeter saw in the unbared womb of Baubo."[8] One version has it that she saw Iakchos there. "A special epiphany of the god was expressed in the name Iakchos: it was both a name and a shout of invocation," a birth in speech.[9] Iakchos, the name that the bacchantes cry out, is a name for Dionysos, but Baubo is not the mother of Dionysos. She holds in her womb not Dionysos but the name of Dionysos. Demeter sees not Dionysos but a cry. With her, we see the cry. We see the presence of writing in speech. The woman with the empty womb is filled, in the myth, by her own laughter at Baubo's revelation. It is not corporeal fertility alone, but a broader creative authority, that the sight of Baubo restores to Demeter. She sees the presence of an absence: not what is but what is yet to be.

What did Nietzsche see when he looked into Baubo? Iakchos, we are told, is another name for Dionysos. Is Nietzsche calling us to witness his birth posthumously? Certainly something of Nietzsche can be seen in Baubo.

One need not see Nietzsche—or Iakchos—in Baubo. Perhaps when Baubo lifted her skirts there was nothing there at all—nothing, that is, but Baubo: the place of woman's sexuality, the emptiness from which something may come.

Nietzsche gave the name of Baubo to Truth and named Truth a woman "who has reasons for not letting us see her reasons." In doing so, he alluded to presence of a reason beyond reason, that is, of reason beyond rationality. Nietzsche's "We are all philologists now," which at first appears to confine us to the text, moves us beyond as well as within it. The substitution of philology for philosophy opposes the philologist to the logician as the philosopher was opposed to the sophist. By looking at the words themselves, we come to see the conditions, contracts, and the constructions of women on which they are written. The gesture of Baubo throws back at Nietzsche the critique of the nymph Echo.

What lies behind knowledge, reason, behind language? It is lack, or as Rousseau said in *On the Origin of Language,* it is desire.[10] The apprehension that the sight of lack produces in men is no less evident here. As we have become more reflective, more self-conscious, concerning the origins of our historical moment and our conceptions of authority, we have increasingly become preoccupied by the connection between sexuality and language. The central debates of our time, in politics and in the academy, concern these and their points of intersection.

Baubo and the Medusa are not merely images of lack nor of the reduction of women to the mark of their sexuality, to the capacities of their bodies. Nor are they images of power, distorted or misread. They are images of difference and contradiction, opposed to the stable dictate, the governing word. They serve as the linchpin of systems of authority, the juncture of word and flesh, the pivot whereby one turns into the other. Nietzsche's momentary and allusive unveiling of Baubo marks the advent of another such revaluation.

Ancient myth and classical philosophy share a sexed response to lack, to the absence of closure, to power in the body, and to the recognition of women's sexuality as a site of authority. The sight of Baubo, the site of truth, produces embarrassed silence in men and children, fertility in women. The sight of the Gorgon produces paralysis in men, confirming power in women. Reading Nietzsche, or Foucault, or Derrida, or any of those whose faith in closure is suspect produces the effects of the Medusa in the agents and beneficiaries of the rational legal order. Men claim that such insights leave them paralyzed, unable to act effectively in the political world. They are made impotent by the sight of lack.

This critique of poststructuralism, with its covert mythic referents and ill-concealed fears that the author may be deprived of a conventional primacy, is followed by a peculiarly ironic reassurance. No one need fear poststructuralism, we are told, because nothing will come of it. It is, commentators emphasize, marking it with the signs of a customary feminine inferiority, merely a fashion.

The identification of clothing with women marks them as having something to hide. Fashion is something women use to conceal their lack. Like all such veils, it calls attention to that which it purports to hide. The identification of poststructuralism with fashion recalls the construction of women as lacking and marks poststructuralism as possessed of this same feminine lack. What poststructuralists lack, in this scheme, is the phallus. The identification of poststructuralism with political impotence owes more to the cultural construction of woman as castrated and the cluster of metaphors that proceed from this than it does to either empirical estimates of the influence or efficacy of poststructuralists or to analyses of the consequences of their propositions.

The metonymic effects of the image of Baubo (in the absence of closure) are, however, not limited to the opponents of poststructuralism; they are happily appropriated by poststructuralists, who seem to regard the metaphor as apt enough. Poststructuralism knows lack as its source. Irigaray's attention to Plato's *hystera;* Derrida's attention to being as absence; Lacan's attention to the mother's phallus, the place of absence in which nothing is present, but from which humanity proceeds; and the reflections in Cixous, in Lacan, in Kristeva, in Irigaray, in Derrida, and in Foucault on the powers of desire are speculations on lack. Like the lack that is their metaphor, they have been productive. The silence of women became, in these texts, that which "speaks in the other." The revelation the feminine lack became the annunciation of the word in woman, and a revelation of feminine capacity. The direction of the gaze onto Baubo restored fertility to a generation of women. The recognition by women of their sexuality made this absence a presence, this lack replete.

The women's sex figures in tradition and modernity as a sign of inferiority, of the lack of power, and as the occasion for subjection. The sight of Baubo speaks to Nietzsche of the centrality of women to truth, or, let us say, to philosophy, to philology, to self-knowledge. The construction of these systems inscribes feminine sexuality as cipher and sign. The mark of the feminine is the zero in this schema, the sign of lack, the emptiness at the center that, once added to another, increases it tenfold.

# 17
## The Laughter of Sarah

The fables of Sarah and Hannah, Mary and Elizabeth belong to a different mystery cycle, another moment in the order of word and flesh. In these, the coming of the new covenant is accomplished by filling an empty womb with speech. Sarah greets the new order with the laughter of Demeter; Elizabeth greets it with the speech of revelation.

Sarah was a woman "well-stricken in age; it had ceased to be with Sarah after the manner of women." Sarah was, like Demeter, barren, and a wanderer. But Sarah's child is the product of the logos. She conceives through the prayers of men and the declarations of the deity.

The Lord said to Abram "I will make your descendants as the dust of the earth; so that if one can count the dust of the earth your descendants also can be counted."[1] Later a still childless Abram asks, "'O Lord God, what wilt thou give me, for I continue childless, and the heir of my house is Eliezer of Damascus.' . . . And the word of the Lord came to him, 'This man shall not be your heir; your own son shall be your heir.'" This child is conceived in the mind: from the word of God in the ear of Abram. "And he believed the Lord; and he reckoned it to him as righteousness."[2]

Abraham's faith in the word is associated with the possession of land, an almost infinite dissemination of his name—the name of the father, temporal greatness, and an enduring covenant. When Abram first obeys the word of God and leaves his own country, he is told, "And I will make of you a great nation."[3] With the promise of descendants comes the promise of property "for all the land which you see I will give to you and to your descendants."[4] God gives Abraham a history with these descendants.

> Then the Lord said to Abram, "Know of a surety that your descendants will be sojourners in a land that is not theirs, and will be slaves there, and will be oppressed for four hundred years; but I will bring judgement on the nation which they serve, and afterward they will come out with great possessions."[5]

The word of God will bring Abram not only a child but time and property, not only a covenant but the name of the father.

> No longer shall your name be Abram, but your name shall be Abraham, for I have made you the father of a multitude of nations. I will make you exceedingly fruitful; and I will make nations of you, and kings shall come forth from you. And I will establish my covenant between me and you and your descendants.[6]

The annunciation of the covenant is accompanied by a rewriting of the names of Abraham and Sarah. Abraham is to inscribe the covenant on the phallus, on his body and the bodies of his people.[7] This inscription of the word of the Lord on the phallus marks Abraham's progeny as children of the covenant, of the word. Covenant replaces blood in the constitution of a people yet to come.

The child of Abraham's flesh would require additional annunciations. The last was meant for Sarah's ear.

> They said to him, "Where is your wife?" And he said, "She is in the tent." The Lord said, "I will return to you in the spring and your wife shall have a son." And Sarah was listening at the tent door behind him.[8]

Abraham had heard the word of the Lord with faith. Sarah laughs. "And Sarah laughed within herself, saying; 'After I am waxed old shall I have pleasure, my lord being old also?'" Sarah's laughter is associated in the text with her desire, pleasure in a woman's body, and a certain skepticism regarding both the word of the Lord and the power of the phallus. The Lord rebukes her laughter, and "she was afraid."[9] In this text, the word overcomes the body, men overcome women, fear overcomes laughter, and faith overcomes a reasoned skepticism.

This is one of the repeated annunciations, the repeated conceptions, of the rule of the logos. This is the long advent of the order of the word. The rebuke to Sarah's laughter speaks of a change in that which stands apart from the word. Sarah is moved from laughter to fear by the word of God. She too will be occupied, she too will conceive according to the word. But while she stands in doubt and opposition she may not laugh, she must be afraid. The absence of words is to be the space of fear. For Sarah, before the word of God, the space outside the word of God could accommodate the opening of wonder, of skepticism and power and happiness. Rebuked by God, she learns that the space outside the word is the space of fear. But there is still a little room in Sarah (in Sarah's mouth, in Sarah's womb) for the absence of words as the presence of pleasure, of joy, of an improbable conception.

Elizabeth's child is described in the text as the product of the penetration of Zechariah's prayers to the ear of the deity: "Do not be afraid, Zechariah; your prayer has been heard: your wife Elizabeth will bear you a son, and you shall name him."[10] Zechariah's refusal to believe in the power of the word of the Lord to overcome the body is punished by rendering him mute. "Behold, you will be silent and unable to speak until the day that these things come to pass, because you did not believe my words."[11] The space outside the word, the space of skepticism and the concerns of the body, has become a place of exile and subjection.

The priority of writing to speech in the logos is inscribed in the relation of Zechariah to the child. After the child's birth, Elizabeth declares that he is to be called John, but her words are powerless. Speech returns to Zechariah when he inscribes the name the Lord assigned the child. They turn to the father. "And he asked for a writing tablet and wrote, 'His name is John.' And they all marveled."[12]

The prophetic capacities of the child Elizabeth conceives are given first to her. "Now as soon as Elizabeth heard Mary's greeting, the child leaped in her womb and Elizabeth was filled with the Holy Spirit, and cried aloud."[13] Neither her body nor her voice remain within her power, subject to her will. She is occupied by prophecy and the Holy Spirit: by the word, the male, the abstract. The child in her womb is the prophet of new order. "In the beginning was the Word."

The gospel of John claims all creation and procreation for the Word, and names that word masculine.

Through him all things came to be; not one thing had its being but through him. All that came to be had life in him.[14]

One is called not to believe in the incarnate God, but in "the name of him."

> Who was born not out of human stock or urge of the flesh or will of man but of God himself.[15]

The exchange of word for flesh, of dictat for desire, of the word of God for the will of man, underwrites the New Testament.

Paintings of the Annunciation conventionally show Mary reading at the moment of conception. She is occupied by words: the spoken (sometimes the written) words of dove or angel, the text before her. Later commentators would claim that Mary had conceived not through her sex but through her ear, as annunciation may lead to conception.

The word whispered in the ear begets not only flesh but more words. The progeny given to Abraham are accompanied by the texts of the covenant that will be written on their bodies. The word of the Lord that answers the prayers of Zechariah conceives not only a child but a prophet, not only a prophet but a series of prophecies. The angel prophesies to Zechariah. Elizabeth prophesies as she bears the child in her womb. John prophesies. Before she brings forth the child, Mary will bring forth the words of the Magnificat. Samuel, who listened in the dark, will prophesy.

Samuel was born to Hannah, a barren woman. "The Lord had closed her womb," but she prayed "and the Lord remembered her." She brings the child to the temple, accompanied by a prayer that Mary will echo in the Magnificat. Samuel will anoint David. The rule of the word, the words of the prophets, and the fulfilment of prophecy come from the triumph of the word over the failure of the flesh.

The word penetrates men's bodies as easily as the bodies of women. The word enters the ears of Abraham and writes itself in his conceptions and upon his body and the bodies of his descendants. Jeremiah declares, "The word of the Lord came to me saying, 'Before I formed you in the womb I knew you.'"

> Then the Lord put forth his hand and touched my mouth; and the Lord said to me, "Behold I have put my words in your mouth. See I have set you this day over nations and over kingdoms, to pluck up and to break down."[16]

The power of the word was linked, for the prophets as for Abraham, to temporal power. That power was sweet in the mouth.

"You, son of man hear what I say to you; be not rebellious like that rebellious house; open your mouth and eat what I give you." And when I looked, behold a hand was stretched out to me and, lo, a written scroll was in it . . . and he said to me, "Son of man, eat what is offered to you; eat this scroll, and go, speak to the house of Israel." So I opened my mouth, and he gave me the scroll to eat. And he said to me, "Son of man, eat this scroll that I give you and fill your stomach with it." Then I ate it; and it was in my mouth as sweet as honey.[17]

Ezekiel submits to God, fills his mouth with that which God gives him, and he prophesies. The mouth becomes the feminine sex, now inscribed on a man's body. The man's body becomes the womb of the word.

The myth of Demeter, as the Greeks told it, was a simple one. Once there was a barren woman, wandering. She saw another woman's sex. She laughed, and she became fertile. This story of laughter and conception is altered in the story of Sarah. There too, we are told, was a barren woman, wandering. But she does not come to Baubo's flesh. The word of God is brought to her, or rather, to her husband. She too laughs, but she is rebuked. She is the first in these stories to bear a son in fulfilment of the word. The myth of Sarah exchanges the word for the flesh, man for woman, the ear for the eye, fear for laughter, the divine text for the earthly body.

Scriptural myths tell this story many times. The story of Hannah makes mother and child the womb of the word: the earthly mother's flesh becomes the divine father's prophecy. The story of Ezekiel takes not only laughter but speech from the skeptical. The story of Mary, the culmination of this cycle of myths, echoes the story of Sarah, for this is the founding of another covenant. In this story, the word is returned to the woman, in her ear, in her mouth, in her womb. She brings forth the word from her flesh. Irigaray will return to this site and conceive by looking into this woman's flesh.

For Freud, the sight of Baubo remains the site of fear. In Freud's myth there was once a man who saw the woman's sex, the sex of the other. He was frightened. He sees that women are maimed and impotent. He fears that he might be made maimed and impotent. He begins to plot against his father, the powerful one who could do these things.

The stories of the children of Abraham turn on an exchange of fear for laughter, a lack revealed for a power revealed, impotence for fertility, feminine subjection for feminine power, a male viewer for a female one. In these stories, a cycle of fertility and generation is exchanged for a cycle of violence and death. But not all men see Baubo in the same way. Another man who was and was not Dionysos, who was and was not the Crucified, he stood before the other and did not unveil her. She lifted up her skirts for him, and he saw himself in her.

# 18
## The Annunciation: The Text of the Womb

A s Nietzsche looked into Baubo, so Irigaray looks into Plato: Plato's womb, Plato's *hystera*. This is the site of Plato's cave, of an imperfect but revolutionary apprehension. This is the site of conception, the place from which unlooked-for beings are brought forth. This is the place of Socrates the midwife, who recognized those who had conceived and delivered them of the conceptions they labored to bring forth. Irigaray, like Socrates, sees Plato full of improbable conceptions. Look, after Socrates, after Nietzsche, into the empty womb with the speculum of another woman and see what may have been conceived in that space.

Irigaray's reading of Plato reveals the willingness of the poststructuralists to enter the canon as the canon enters them. She, like Lacan, reads Plato more carefully, more respectfully, more thoroughly, than those who purport to honor him, for she read without excising the myths and the jokes that embarrass too many contemporary philosophers. She reads more critically and thus more filially. "All those who go on their own way carry my image too into the breaking day."[1]

Irigaray's looking, like Nietzsche's and like ours, comes in the light of another myth, the myth of the Annunciation. The question "What comes before the word?" puts both Christian and philosophic structures in question.

What does the womb mean?

We have heard, often enough (the ear is the only orifice that cannot be closed) what the phallus means. The phallus is the instrument of sexual differentiation, the sign of power. On it, with it, is written the name of the father. The phallus is an instrument of authority: political and literary, the authority of representation, the authority of incarnation. The phallus is not an organ, but a sign taken for an ascription of power. The phallus serves as a pole: orienting the drives. In the phallus the power of the word becomes manifest in the flesh. Political and literary authority, the power of the word and the power of the flesh are now confounded. We recognize that we have our being in language. We find ourselves in the intimate: in the intimate connection of that authority to sexuality and sexual hierarchy, in the partial constitution of the body.

We will find ourselves in utero as well, in the topography of this *antre,* this opening. There are forces here as well: not oriented at a pole but drawn into a vortex. This has been constituted for us as the site of disorder, of the absence of authority and the lack of meaning.

The question "What does the womb mean?" is, like the question it echoes, "What do women want?" already answered, and already answered incorrectly. "As regards little girls, we can say of them that they feel greatly at a disadvantage owing to their lack of a big visible penis, that they envy boys for possessing one and that, in the main for this reason, they develop a wish to be a man." The passage shows the misdirection of thought: from institutions to the individual, from power to the psyche, and it reveals, in the undercurrents of Freud's phrasing, the linkage of women's subjection to the word. Thus Freud writes "we can say of them" and observes that it is the visibility, and thus the legibility, of the penis as signifier that prompts feminine envy and subjection.[2] The womb is already inscribed as the site that is without meaning, the sight of horror and aphasia, the unspeakable, the absence of speech and the absence of desire. Women are already inscribed as wanting, lacking. This inscription, which pretends to strip things bare, conceals within it the contradictory truth upon which it depends. Difference is met with horror, and with desire. Lack is the impulse to desire, and wanting the engine of the will. Freud's reading of the boy's horror at the sight of the mother's sex is correct twice: once in his reading, and once again in his silence. The horror at the recognition of the woman as lacking a phallus veils the horror at the child's recognition of his own lack. The boy sees that the woman does not have what he has, that she is lacking. Behind this recognition of difference as lack is another. The fear that fills the boy is not, as Freud averred, simply fear of what may happen to him and horror at what has happened to another. The fear of what he may become veils the fearful recognition of what he already is: other to those he regarded as his own. The horror at the sight of difference in another veils the horrible sight of his own difference.

This is the fear that haunts our dreams and stories: the one in the mother's form who is not the mother but a threat, the man in the father's body who is not the father, the occupied bodies of Ripley, pod people, and Stepford wives, the murderer concealed in the house, the alien hidden in the viscera, the image in the mirror that commands rather than obeys. In these we recall hesitantly, allusively, the recognition that those we thought were like ourselves, that we might know and be known by, are alien to us. The thoughts we cannot touch, the sensations we cannot feel, the sentiments we cannot share take form in these.

This is a fear of lack, a fear of the other, a fear that one might become other to oneself. This is a fear of loss, of the loss of language, or a language sufficient to overcome the isolation of the flesh. This is a fear of aphasia: that the sight of lack will not give birth to desire, to will. This is a fear that the cry to the other will be answered only by silence.

That which was presented to us as a moment of closure, in which the male child entered into stable categories and a sturdy, if conventional, hierarchy and fixed his sexual identity, is not the achievement of closure but the opening into indeterminacy. Hidden within it is the unsettling recognition of difference in oneself and one's own.

Ours is the sex that is not one: not a sex, not one sex, but many. This is the organ that is not an organ, the sex that is not one sex but the site of diverse fragmented parts. The womb is one part: a partial locus of feminine sexuality. This allusive space becomes metonymic for Irigaray, comprising, comprehending—and concealing—feminine sexuality. Irigaray's conception of feminine sexuality is partial here: incomplete, partial to the woman, partial to the reading of woman as mother (or, rather, as the place from which others come). She speaks, but she is blind.

If we are to find our way out of the not quite closed place in which we find ourselves, Plato's *hystera* is a good place to start. The womb is marked for us as the site of our corporeal origins.

The phallus is external. It disseminates. The womb is the mythic site of the internal. Exploration of the womb identified with exploration of the interior—of what? In looking into this womb we are to explore the body and the possibility of conception—of thought, of reflection, and of enlightenment—within it. This interior is not easily seen. It is enfolded in the flesh and lies in darkness. If it is not invisible, it at least requires a speculum. Looking into the womb is not (as Irigaray repeated) like looking in the mirror. The womb is not a sight that must be, will inevitably be, seen. Rather, it is a site that one must make an effort to see. This sight is hidden in the body. This site is hard to see, in part, because (as we shall see) it is the place where (and the apparatus whereby) things are made.

The phallus is, for us, the visible site of the logos: of the word, the law, and the drive of writing. This is the embodiment of the drive to writing: writing and written. This is the site of authority, political and literary. Irigaray's speculations—like Plato's, Nietzsche's, and Lacan's—are, as her opening paragraph suggests, metaphysical. They are speculations on—and over, beyond, and beneath—the body and that which underwrites it.

This is part of the body's overcoming in the fullest sense. The triumph of logos over the bodies of women is overcome by the reappearance and reassertion of the body.[3] The silencing of the laughter of Sarah is answered with the laughter of the Medusa. The authoritative closure of the male body (an authorial fiction, and an authoritative one) is ruptured in the analysis of Plato's hystera. The veiling of Baubo is undone by another woman, who takes up the speculum. As in all such overcomings, that which is overcome remains, not only as the precursor of the overcoming but as its author.

Irigaray offered a "silent prescription." She, like Freud, pretended to the therapeutic, but she looked for redemption not in speech or in writing but in that which is said to be prior to both. She looked to that which underwrites speech. In another sense, however, this is a rejection of the methods as well as the content of psychoanalysis, that most phallologocentric of discourses. Irigaray questioned not only the centrality of the phallus but that of the logos. The rejection of the talking cure challenged the privileged methods of the canon: the linear form of discourse, dialogue, and dialectic. Irigaray thus offered a prescription in the full sense. She turns, therapeutically, to that which comes before writing. She looks to that on which and within the limits of which things are written, the site where authority is exercised. Plato, Nietzsche, Lacan, and Irigaray gesture, in language, to something beyond and before it. The gesture is familiar, but it has not grown less evocative with use.

Socrates made his hearers pregnant through the ear and, making himself midwife, delivered them through the mouth. Derrida found himself in Rousseau's silences, and in filling those silences occupied Rousseau. Irigaray found her authority in the womb of Plato and in the wombs of Nietzsche and Lacan: as child, as lover, and as that which they conceived but did not bring forth.

Traditional readings of Plato held that the cave was an image of error. The mythic image captured not only the distortions that belong to the imperfections of human apprehension but those that belong to representation. Irigaray read the classic message of the cave on the surface of Lacan's mirror. In her reading, the mirror stage becomes a moment of fraud and deception.[4] Irigaray read Lacan as reproducing the "dream of symmetry" between being and language. She saw a "desire for likeness" in Lacan: a desire for the recognition of others as one's own, and the desire for the likeness of representations to the represented.

This reading, which remained on the surface of the text, did Lacan an injustice. Lacan's myth acknowledged the inadequacy of the image. One can easily open Lacan's account and read in it an insistence on the partiality of the image.[5] The image is seen as apart from oneself, set out in the external world. The self seen in the mirror is two-dimensional, superficial, a surface. And yet this image is a part of oneself. Though it stands outside and apart from the reach of the hand or the sensations of the body, it is nevertheless responsive to the will. The will and the eye take it for one's own.

Lacan's account is revelatory because one can read in it the effects of the entry into language. The self that is taken for one's own is apart from oneself, the basis for an identification with others, and a text, written on a flat surface: a sign of what it is to be one of a kind. Lacan identifies the acquisition of language, the alienation and recognition of oneself, and this migration of the will into the sign as met with *jouissance,* with satisfaction.

The mirror, however, is only one means of representation. Irigaray's myth brings others, the cave and the womb, before us. Her myth sees the representative apparatus as productive, and in this her account surpasses the Platonic. This site, this sight, is productive not only of the self but of many images. Lacan's myth makes us our own authors—or rather, it makes us appear to ourselves as authors. Irigaray's mythic sojourn in Plato's womb makes those contained in the womb effects, involved in the creation of the image (though not willfully) and having it imposed on them. In Irigaray's myth, conceiving the self, conceiving oneself, is a more collective activity, and a less willful one. This is another move away from the faith of the Enlightenment in the I.

Irigaray is engaged in thinking woman apart from man. And so she, in this order of the word and the flesh, in the moment of the critique of phallologocentrism, thinks woman in relation to the word. She invokes the Annunciation, only to subject it to the critique of the nymph Echo. Irigaray is the woman bearing the word within her, the word that will become flesh. She is the woman man has not occupied, who will bring forth the new order. Irigaray's invocation of the Christian myth of annunciation and incarnation inverts it. Authority resides not in the word but in the flesh, not in the seed but in the womb.

For Irigaray, as for commentators on an earlier French revolution, the language of revolution is the arcana of the eternal feminine, the Gothic mystery of the womb. She is "the one who has lived more experiences than any single man. She who counted one by one the beatings of your hearts, and your fathers' hearts. . . . The old deep mid-night to whom one cannot speak aloud in the daytime."[6] Irigaray embraces the writing of woman as flesh, woman as mother, woman as womb. The woman keeps the body, remains of the body, enfolds the body of the other within her. "Whenever that question, 'Where is my body?' is reborn in you, what do you do but go right back to digging in the earth who has always kept it for you."[7] Irigaray is mindful of the claim that writing is an all too male autoeroticism, a transgression through which men escape the name of the father, and the commands of nature, to take the body in hand and subject it to the will. For her, as for Derrida, "the supplement that 'cheats' maternal 'nature' operates as writing, and as writing it is dangerous to life."[8] The desire of writing, in writing, is to make a world apart from and beyond nature, to acquire authority over the body, to overcome the body. For Irigaray, this undertaking invests the sacramental phrase "This is my body" with irony and nostalgia. "When you say: 'This is my body,' how is this ultimate thought fomented? . . . And is it too late for you to do that? Haven't you spent your life despising what you now want most?"[9] Yet this phrase is less an utterance than an exchange. The priest who holds up the host and says "This is my body" speaks in the name of the father. He holds not his own body but the sign of the body of God, which is to be transubstantiated, becoming the body of God itself. This body will enfold him and the bodies of the faithful. But this is, for the faithful, the means to both life in the world to come and the resurrection of the body. The sign that stands of and for the body is seen as the means to its epiphany.

For Irigaray, the sacrament is inverted. Divinity rests not in the Child of Man but in the Mother of God, not in the word that impregnates the womb but in the womb itself, in that which lies under, before, and beyond the word. The declaration "This is my body" refuses the complete, ecstatic incorporation into the world of signs. The passionate union that dissolves the boundaries between the bodies of the faithful, between the human and the divine, and between the world of scripture and the desire of the body for its own continuance is refused as well. In Irigaray's mouth, as in Cixous's, the declaration "This is my body" carries a defense of difference and particularity. Likeness appears in the particularity of bodies, the indissoluble separateness, the perfect privacy of pleasure and pain. "Different bodies, that no doubt makes the likeness."[10]

Before the word, woman is that on which the word is written. "I even had to scrape my woman's flesh clean of the insignia and marks you had etched upon it."[11] The feminine stands behind and before the sign, and remains beyond it. "There is nothing like unto women. They go beyond all simulation. And when they are copied the abyss remains." The feminine is that which is not wholly knowable, not wholly comprehensible. "Her ultimate depth never returns to the light of day."[12]

# 19
## The Circumcised

Circumcision, the ceremony that makes the phallus the privileged site of scripture, the site of writing and the mark of the chosen, also makes the phallus the place where scripture fails and the body triumphs. This site, where the word is written on the body, is at once weapon and wound, sign and stigma. From this small drawing of blood much writing and much blood will flow. On this site of founding and inauguration, much will come to an end.

This is a scandalous place, and a place of deference to convention. Derrida, recording the convention of his bris, of his own inclusion in the covenant, writes of his mother

> sucking up the blood through a lightweight cloth, the tight filter of a dressing around the penis, on the seventh day, when they would put on orange-flower water in Algeria.[1]

Derrida's account recalls the act not of Abraham but of Zipporah,

> the one who repaired the failing of a Moses incapable of circumcising his own son, before telling him, "You are a husband of blood to me," she had to eat the bloody foreskin, I imagine first by sucking it.[2]

In this sacred inversion of the sacred, the mohel becomes a woman rather than a man. Consummation is accomplished not by the man penetrating the woman's sex but by the woman penetrating the man's sex. It is the man's blood rather than the woman's that seals the marriage; it is the man who is bound to the woman. In this consummation, it is the man who feels pain and the woman who inflicts it.

Freud's myth is inverted as well. In this totem meal it is not the sons who consume bits of the father but the mother, "my beloved cannibal," who consumes a bit of the son.[3] Here the beloved is not the consumed but the one who consumes. Here it is not the mother but the father who is absent. The son who left the mother's sex becomes the son whose sex enters the mother's mouth. Masculine is exchanged for feminine pain—and pleasure. And, on the cover, the duplicitous image of the author is inverted, and in this inversion the hands of the author meet in the mimicry of the woman's sex. So too, in the text, do the hands of the son describe a mother whose sex holds the son. So too does the mother's sex come to bear the mark of the son she bore, inscribed with his name, his authority.

Circumcision thus enables Derrida to keep a part from Geoffrey Bennington. "This book presupposes a contract," writes the ambivalent, anonymous narrator who opens *Jacques Derrida*. By that contract, "G.B. undertook to describe, according to the pedagogical and logical norms to which he holds, if not the totality of J.D.'s thought, then at least the general system of that thought." Bennington would give order, system, and closure to Derrida's work. But "what is at stake in J.D.'s work is to show how any such system must remain essentially open." The contract, therefore, "stipulated that J.D., having read G.B.'s text, would write something escaping the proposed systematization, surprising it."[4]

Circumcision becomes the rite through which Derrida fulfills the contract by evading its governance. Derrida can satisfy the terms of the contract only if he evades it. He will fulfill it only insofar as he remains outside the authority of the order established within it. Derrida's presence in the text is secured by the manifestation of the text's inability to contain him. And yet it is the text itself that calls for and calls forth this evasion, that incites it and makes it possible. Circumcision becomes what it has always been: the writing that opens. In this inscription on the flesh, the flesh is opened to the word. This is the violence of the letter, perhaps, but it is also a strategy whereby the incarnate, the embodied, evades comprehension in the text.

If Derrida evaded Geoffrey Bennington's authority—partially—he did not wholly retain his own. The son was not to be the only one to write on his circumcision, or on the veiled lips of the Algerian woman. Luce Irigaray's account of the circumcised entitled "Veiled Lips" speaks against Derrida's at every point. For Irigaray, circumcision remains the end of the flesh, "the body's entry into the world of signs." Circumcision remains Jewish, masculine, authoritative, "the opening onto the stage of sameness."[5] In circumcision, "the Jew agrees to take on the actor's role," which he can afford "since he has already paid for it." Nietzsche, she observes, regarded the Jew as "a born 'man of letters'" and an actor.[6] "And rightly so," she adds; "circumcision attests to a specialist's expertise in the field of signs."[7] In these passages, Irigaray aligns the Jew with representation, the sign, the mark, the play of utility and duplicity in accounting. "The spot left by the Jew is still there. To make him play it over again as a simulacrum is worth more. Provided he is made to pass as other. And without a veil?" Irigaray is reluctant to permit the son to "pass as other." It is not as Algerian nor as Jew but as woman that the mother is foreign.

Irigaray, reading Nietzsche's claim that "nothing is more foreign to woman than truth" with the passage "her great art is falsehood, her chief concern is appearance and beauty," argues that to write this "is surely to say the same thing twice, with the exception that one word has been forgotten the second time, the word 'foreign.'" Neither women nor "falsehood nor appearance nor beauty are 'foreign' to truth," Irigaray argues, yet the relation of women to truth is concealed. Irigaray sees her task as that of a late Enlightenment, stripping away the veils, unbinding the veiled lips, unwinding "the shroud of your indifference." Truth is naked to Irigaray.

> I have washed off your masks and makeup, scrubbed away your multicolored projections and designs, stripped off your veils and wraps that hid the shame of your nudity. I have even had to scrape my woman's flesh clean of the insignia and marks you had etched upon it.[8]

Draupadi's triumph was to remain clothed and inviolate, to unfurl the continuous text that held her at the center. Irigaray would strip not only herself but all others, "tearing those dearly won shrouds of glory away from you rag by rag."[9] Truth is in the flesh, for Irigaray, but we are not all equal under, or in, the skin. The other is wholly other.

"There is nothing like unto women," Irigaray writes. "They go beyond all simulation."[10] The son cannot, in Irigaray's account, speak of the mother, hold the mother in the text. "Among, between, the veils of the one, of the other, some misunderstanding may still, at times, subsist." For "she is unable to talk about herself as he does."[11]

Irigaray sets the duplicities of Derrida's myth of origin against the sex that is not one, his all too literary duplicities against the limiting horizon of sex. Yet Derrida does not see sex as a horizon but as a play of representation, not as the body against the word but as a series of iridescent transubstantiations. Perhaps the desire to pass is not to be condemned.

Derrida writes of circumcision as a site of contradiction, "that wound that I have never seen," the site that is not a sight. This is the place of the word for and against the body: the word that has authority over the body, the word that gives the body power. This is the site of the power given and taken away. This is the phallus wounded and empowered. Derrida senses

> the pain which I suppose to be nil and infinite, and I can still feel
> it, the phantom burning, in my belly, irradiating a diffuse zone
> around the sex, a threat which returns every time the other is in pain,
> if I identify with him, with her even, with my mother especially.[12]

The letter is a gate, an opening, a wound. The phallus, inscribed with the name of the father (perhaps, in a single gesture, with all the uncountable names of God), opens the child to the mother. Derrida recognizes in the small excision the great loss that commitment to a people entails. The demand for the proofs of love, for endless sacrifice that politics requires is refigured here. The gift of a part, the gift of the self, that binds one to the whole leaves one open to the other. In Derrida's "circonfession," the sign of the Jews becomes the sacrament of the Christians; circumcision becomes transubstantiation. The circumcised foreskin becomes the Eucharist. The pain that opens one to the other is acknowledged as an imagined memory, lacked and desired.

Derrida's desire brings us back to Isaac and Abraham, to the evasion that fulfills the contract.

The covenant between Abraham and God is sealed not by Abraham's sacrifice of Isaac but by the evasion of that sacrifice. Isaac becomes the absence of an absence. As he is conceived, he becomes the absence of the absence of a child in Sarah's womb. With his birth, he becomes the absence of the absence of Abraham's posterity, the overcoming of a mortal lack. When the word holds back the father's hand, Isaac becomes the absence of his own absence, the sign of a contract fulfilled in its evasion. Circumcision is the sign of the dissemination that would make Abraham the father of a people too great to be numbered, an absence of flesh that presents itself as a deferral, a debt that will be repaid many times.

In circumcision, in bearing the mark that is an opening and a scar, in the maintenance of the rite of opening, Derrida is marked as Jew and as poststructuralist. In the acclamation of Jesus Christ as the Messiah,

Christianity gives closure. In Christ the contract is fulfilled, time comes to an end. Christian anti-Semitism opposes itself to the Jewish denial of that closure. The denial of Christ is the denial of closure. Judaism remains aligned with indeterminacy and aporia. The dissemination of Abraham's limitless progeny continues. Time continues, the contract continues its inexorable demands, and, perhaps, authority answers the proofs of love with the grace of evasion.

If Derrida's desire brings us back to Isaac and to Abraham, to the evasion that fulfills the contract, perhaps it also brings us back to the laughter of Sarah. In the children of Abraham, the woman's skeptical laughter becomes the father's faith in the word and is made flesh. For them, the ear is almost but not quite the womb, the father almost but not quite the mother. The contract is written in the ear, on the empty womb, in laughter silenced, in the raised hand holding the knife. The sacrifice is almost demanded but not quite, the contract almost but not quite fulfilled. The laughter of Demeter echoes in the laughter of Sarah, the laughter of Sarah in the laughter of the Medusa. We await the Messiah.

# Notes

## INTRODUCTION

1. Louis Althusser and Etienne Balibar, *Reading Capital*, trans. Ben Brewster (London: Verso 1997) 16.

## CHAPTER 1

1. Some years ago, I had a very lively and pleasant conversation on this subject with John Pocock, who disagreed with me completely, arguing that Cromwell referred only to Charles Stuart's acts of violence. For Pocock, the meaning of the words is bounded by Cromwell's intent and the historical moment in which they were first uttered. I would not confine meaning to intent, and that the reach of Cromwell's words was broader than his intent. I contend that the words "Man of Blood" reveal the meanings immanent in them over time, in the hearing of those many generations removed from the time of their first utterance.
2. Carolyn Walker Bynum, *Jesus as Mother* (Berkeley: University of California Press, 1982).
3. *French Caricature*, figure 1, 37.
4. Machiavelli, *Discourses*, trans. Leslie Walter (New York: Penguin Books, 1983), III:6. I have given the story, not as it appears in the *Discourses*, but as I first heard it in graduate school, where the story was passed from one generation to the next. I have also heard it told by my former colleague at Princeton, Maurizio Viroli, a son of Forli, who tells it very well indeed. One of the most interesting aspects of this story (in our time) is that which makes it most shocking: its rejection of the primacy of maternity and the subordination of the mother's interests to her children. The story was a favorite of Machiavelli, who cites it in *Discourses*, in *Florentine Histories* 8:34, and again in *The Prince*, chapter 20. As Hannah Pitkin observes, the story had special force for Machiavelli. "His first diplomatic mission was to her court, and she made a fool of him in the negotiations, finally dismissing him while she nursed her ailing youngest child." Hannah Pitkin, *Fortune Is a Woman: Gender and Politics in the Thought of Niccolo Machiavelli* (Berkeley: University of California Press, 1984), 249–50.
5. Thomas Hobbes, *De Cive*, chapter 9. See also Carole Pateman's commentary on Hobbes in *The Sexual Contract* (Stanford: Stanford University Press, 1988).
6. Pitkin, *Fortune Is a Woman*, 249–50.

## CHAPTER 2

1. The exclusion of revolutionary women from the institutions of the later revolutionary state has been treated in the work of Joan Scott, Louise Tilly, Maurice Agulhon, Dorinda Outram, and Lynn Hunt.

2. Alexis de Tocqueville, *Democracy in America,* trans. George Lawrence (New York: Harper Collins, 1988), 2:704, 601. Carole Pateman observes in *The Sexual Contract* that the position of the marriage contract in liberal theory and liberal practice rests—when it is presented as voluntary—on a similar paradox of disinterested self-abnegation.

3. Tocqueville, *Democracy in America,* 603.

4. The reading of the woman's body as open does not belong exclusively to liberalism or to modernity, though it acquires a peculiar significance within those systems. Constructions of the woman's body as open on other temporal sites can be found in *Zone* 3, 4, and 5; Julia Kristeva, "Stabat Mater," in *The Kristeva Reader* (160–86); Rudolph Bell, *Holy Anorexia;* and Francis Barker, *The Tremulous Private Body.*

5. Jacques Derrida, *Of Grammatology,* trans. Gayatri Spivak (Baltimore: Johns Hopkins University Press, 19), 134.

6. Rousseau, *Emile,* 359.

7. Hobbes, *Leviathan,* 162.

8. John Locke, *Two Treatises of Government,* ed. Peter Laslett (Cambridge: Cambridge University Press, 1963), First Treatise, section 61.

9. Ibid., section 47.

10. That by "condition" Locke refers to her social rather than natural capacities is made evident in the passages that follow this, in which Locke argues that Mary and Elizabeth, as queens of England, would not have been subjected by marriage to the rule of their husbands. See Pateman, *The Sexual Contract.*

11. The centrality of woman to Rousseau's account of political life has received considerable attention. See Pateman, *The Sexual Contract;* Susan Moller Okin, *Women in Western Political Thought* (Princeton: Princeton University Press, 1979); Joel Schwartz, *The Sexual Politics of Jean-Jacques Rousseau* (Chicago: University of Chicago Press, 1984); and Anne Norton, *Reflections on Political Identity* (Baltimore: Johns Hopkins University Press, 1988), chapter 1, Part II.

12. Jean-Jacques Rousseau, *Discourse on Political Economy,* in *On the Social Contract with Geneva Manuscript and Political Economy,* ed. Roger Masters, trans. Judith Masters (New York: St. Martin's Press, 1978), 210.

13. The claim of moments of feminine incapacity is not made to bear much weight in Rousseau's account. He characterizes these as slight and says, "Where the balance is perfectly equal a straw is enough to tip it" (ibid.).

14. Ibid., 223.

15. See Derrida, *Of Grammatology,* part II, and my commentary in *Reflections,* 30–33.

16. Sigmund Freud describes Darwin's account in *Totem and Taboo,* trans. James Strachey (New York: W. W. Norton, 1950), 141.

17. Ibid.

18. Ibid., 140.

19. Ibid., 142 n. 1.

20. Sigmund Freud, *Group Psychology and the Analysis of the Ego,* trans. James Strachey (New York: W. W. Norton, 1959), 54–60.

21. Derrida, *Of Grammatology.*

22. Nietzsche, *The Gay Science,* 38. Nietzsche raises this question again in the preface to *Beyond Good and Evil,* trans. Walter Kaufmann (New York: Vintage Books, 19): "Supposing truth is a woman—what then?"

## CHAPTER 3

1. G. W. F. Hegel, *The Philosophy of History,* trans. J. Sibree (New York: Dover Publications, 1956), 99.

2. Hannah Arendt, *The Origins of Totalitarianism* (New York: Harcourt Brace Jovanovich, 1979), 191.
3. Ibid., 192.
4. Ibid., 192–93.
5. Ibid., Marx quoted in Arendt, *Totalitarianism,* 192.
6. Mill, quoted in Homi Bhabha, "Sly Civility," in *The Location of Culture* (New York: Routledge, 1994), 93. See also Uday Mehta, *Liberalism and Empire* (Chicago: University of Chicago Press, 1999).
7. Bhabha, "Sly Civility," 93.
8. Edward Said, *Orientalism* (New York: Vintage, 1979), 3–4.
9. Stephen Greenblatt has a fine discussion of the *Requerimiento* in *Learning to Curse: Essays in Early Modern Culture* (New York: Routledge, 1992), 26–30.
10. Said, *Orientalism,* 121.
11. Arendt, *Totalitarianism,* 192.
12. Said, *Orientalism,* 119.
13. Albert Memmi, *The Colonizer and the Colonized* (New York: Orion Press, 1965), 119–20.
14. William Shakespeare, *The Tempest,* I.ii.353–67. Stephen Greenblatt discusses this in *Learning to Curse.* It has been a common image since Mannoni.
15. Frantz Fanon, *Black Skin, White Masks,* trans. Charles Lam Markmann (New York: Grove Press, 1967), 18.
16. Ibid., 19.
17. Ibid., 18.
18. Fanon, *Peau noire, masques blancs* (Paris: Editions de Seuil, 1995), 15. The English is available in *Black Skin, White Masks,* 20.
19. Salman Rushdie, *The Satanic Verses* (New York: Viking Penguin, 1989), 3. Homi Bhabha gives a different, and (one relies upon this) fascinating reading of this novel in *The Location of Culture.* This reading foregrounds the relation of postcolonial language to time and nationality.
20. Compare *Midnight's Children* (New York: Knopf, 1981) to *The Satanic Verses.*
21. Rushdie, *The Satanic Verses,* 102.
22. Ibid., 157.
23. Homi Bhabha, "Of Mimicry and Man," in *The Location of Culture* (New York: Routledge, 1994), 86.
24. Ibid.

## CHAPTER 4

1. Roland Barthes, *Mythologies,* trans. Annette Lavers (New York: Hill and Wang, 1957), 116.
2. Robert Frost, "The Gift Outright," poem read at John F. Kennedy's inauguration in 1961. Did the anxieties of empire persist for over two hundred years? After Vietnam, Frost's denial of imperial guilt seems to address both past and future.
3. Edward Said, *Orientalism* (New York: Vintage, 1979), 206.
4. Elaine Showalter, *Sexual Anarchy* (New York: Viking, 1990).

## CHAPTER 5

1. Achille Mbembe, "Provisional Notes on the Postcolony," *Africa* 62, 1 (1992): 7. Mbembe has expanded this analysis in his brilliant book *On the Postcolony* (Berkeley: University of California Press, 2001).
2. "The discourse of post-Enlightenment English colonialism often speaks in a tongue that is forked, not false." Homi Bhabha, "Of Mimicry and Man," in *The Location of Culture* (New York: Routledge, 1994), 85. The distinction is appropriate here as well, for the

aims, intentions, and desires of the post-Enlightenment opponent of the veil are not false but divided against themselves.

3. Albert Memmi, *The Colonizer and the Colonized,* trans. Howard Greenfeld (Boston: Beacon Press, 1967), 132.

4. Ibid., 133.

5. Mbembe, "Provisional Notes," 7.

6. Ibid., 11.

## CHAPTER 6

1. The official publications commemorating the tercentenary of the revolution begin with the acceptance by William and Mary of the rule of England and the Declaration of Rights.

Thus was concluded the central event in the drama that was to become known as the Glorious Revolution of 1688–1689, when a King—James II, who claimed to rule by hereditary, even divine right—was deposed in favor of sovereigns, William III and Mary II, who occupied the throne by the will of the people as expressed through Parliament. *Parliament and the Glorious Revolution 1688–1988,* by Authority of the Lord Chancellor and the Speaker of the House of Commons (London: Her Majesty's Stationery Office, 1988).

2. G. M. Trevelyan, *The English Revolution, 1688–1689* (New York: Henry Holt, 1939), 162. See also *Parliament and the Glorious Revolution 1688–1988.*

3. See Lois Schwoerer's fine study *The Declaration of Rights, 1689* (Baltimore: Johns Hopkins University Press, 1981), especially chapter 5.

4. Anne Stuart to Mary Stuart, letter quoted in Henri van der Zee and Barbara van der Zee, *William and Mary* (London: Macmillan, 1973), 233.

5. Accounts of the warming-pan scandal are legion. See Gilbert Burnet, *Bishop Burnet's History of His Own Time* (Oxford: University Press, 1833), 3:318–23.

6. The stadholderate was hereditary not by law, but in the expectations of the Orange princes and the Dutch republic.

7. Quoted in van der Zee and van der Zee, 91.

8. Thomas Babington Macaulay, *The History of England from the Accession of James II* (1693), 3:228.

9. Burnet, *History,* 3:331, 359. This feature of the invading army is invariably remarked in contemporary accounts.

10. This is a much told story. Burnet's version runs "when they were asked how they could serve in an expedition that was intended to destroy their own religion, one of them answered, his soul was God's but his sword was the Prince of Orange's." *History,* 3:358.

11. "A Dialogue between King William and the Late King James," attributed to Charles Blount, in W. J. Cameron, *Poems on Affairs of State,* 5:235–36 (New Haven: Yale University Press, 1971). It would, of course, be an error to attribute quite this position to William himself.

12. Burnet, *History,* 3:138–39. Mary conferred the crown as the English did, with conditions: "she asked only, that he would obey the command of *Husbands love your wives.*"

## CHAPTER 7

1. G. M. Trevelyan, *The English Revolution 1688–1689* (New York: Henry Holt, 1939), 5.

2. Burke, *Reflections on the Revolution in France* (London: Methuen, 1905), 23.

3. Nietzsche, *On the Genealogy of Morals,* trans. Walter Kaufmann (New York: Vintage, 1969), Second Essay, section 6, 65.

4. David Lagomarsino and Charles Wood, eds. *The Trial of Charles I: A Documentary History,* (Dartmouth, NH: University Press of New England, 1989), 65.

5. Ivan Roots, *The Great Rebellion: 1642–1660* (London: B. T. Batsford, 1966), 70, 72, and chapter 6.

6. Ibid., 81.

7. Carlyle, *Life of Oliver Cromwell* (London: Hutchinson, 1905), 265.

8. Ibid., 49.

9. Ibid., 217 (letter to William Lenthall, speaker of the Parliament, September 4, 1650).

10. Ibid., 116, 117.

11. Ibid., 216, 217 (letter to William Lenthall, speaker of the Parliament, September 4, 1650).

12. Ibid., 156.

13. Ibid., 317–318 (address to Parliament, September 17, 1656).

14. Ibid., 316 (address to Parliament, September 17, 1656).

15. Ibid., 155. Carlyle takes the owl as the totem of philosophy and makes it the frequent object of his derision.

16. Ibid., 265.

17. Ibid., 368.

18. Ibid., 155.

19. Ibid., 158. The Instrument of Government settled the government "in a Single Person and a Parliament." Carlyle describes the instrument (which he, after Cromwell, repeatedly calls "the Thing").

20. Ibid., 368.

21. Ibid., 11.

22. Ibid., 368.

23. Ibid., 11.

24. Ibid., 157.

25. C. V. Wedgwood, *A Coffin for King Charles* (New York: Time Reading Program, 1966), 89, 124.

26. Ibid., 56, 212.

27. Ibid., 213.

28. *Eikon Basilike: The Pourtraicture of His Sacred Majestie in His Solitudes and Sufferings,* facsimile of the 1648 edition (London: Elliot Stock, 1880), 6.

29. "The Female Parricide" in *Poems on Affairs of State,* 5:157. See also "Tarquin and Tulia" (47–54) and "The Duchess of York's Ghost" 5:298–302.

30. Gilbert Burnet, *Bishop Burnet's History of His Own Time* (Oxford: University Press, 1833), 3:406–7.

31. In these phrases, as in other passages, Mary Stuart's intelligence and art are not quite concealed. At such moments one is apprised of the manner in which people exceed the meanings history reads in them.

32. Schwoerer gives a fine account of the ceremony with several significant details, among them William's civilian dress.

33. The "Proclamation of Rights Tableau" was produced by Living Images, and appeared in an exhibition entitled "Parliament and the Glorious Revolution 1688–1689" in the Banqueting House, Whitehall, 1 July–1 October 1988.

## CHAPTER 8

1. Edmund Burke, *Reflections on the Revolution in France* (London: Methuen, 1905), 23.

2. Ibid., 14.

3. Ibid., 19.

4. Ibid., 24. See also 20, 23, 34, 48, 52, 61, 65, 74–75, 90.

5. Burke, *Reflections,* 19.

6. Ibid., 74–75.

7. Thomas Carlyle, *The French Revolution* (Oxford: Oxford University Press, 1989), 1:45.

8. Ibid., 50.

9. Ibid., 52.
10. Ibid., 39.
11. Friedrich Nietzsche, *On the Genealogy of Morals,* trans. Walter Kaufmann (New York: Vintage, 1969), Second Essay, section 4, 62–63.
12. Burke, *Reflections,* 69.
13. Ibid.
14. Ibid., 17.
15. Burke, letter to Lord Charlemont, quoted in Paulson, *Representations of Revolution* (New Haven: Yale University Press, 1983), 57.
16. Burke, Reflections, 119–120.
17. Ibid., 37.
18. Ibid., 27.
19. Ibid., 76, 86.
20. Ibid., 36.
21. Ibid., 17.
22. Ibid., 24.
23. Ibid.
24. Ibid.
25. Ibid.
26. Ibid., 17.
27. Ibid., 39.
28. Ibid., 65.
29. Ibid., 39.
30. Ibid., 76.
31. Ibid.
32. Ibid., 77.
33. Ibid., 77.
34. I am obliged to Uday Mehta, who treats Burke more extensively, more sympathetically, and more profoundly, for this recognition of the importance of psychological wholeness to Burke. For Burke's role as an opponent of colonialism, see Mehta's *Liberalism and Empire* (Chicago: University of Chicago Press, 1999).
35. Burke, *Reflections,* 76.


## CHAPTER 9

1. Simon Schama provides an excellent account of the multiplicity of boundaries, languages, ethnicities and religions among the Dutch. See Simon Schama, *The Embarrassment of Riches: An Interpretation of Dutch Culture in the Golden Age* (New York: Knopf, 1987), especially 54–57 (on boundaries).
2. Owen Felltham, "Brief Character of the Low Countries," quoted in Schama, *Riches,* 265.
3. Andrew Marvell, "The Character Of Holland," in *Satires of Andrew Marvell,* ed. G. A. Aitken (London: George Routledge, 1901), 14–15.
4. Schama, *Riches,* 191.
5. Andrew Marvell, "The Character Of Holland," 16. The imperfect, but perhaps unparalleled, tolerance of religious diversity among the Dutch manifested itself in the prayers for the success of the expedition in 1688. The Amsterdam Portuguese synagogue asked God to "send His Holy Angels to surround with their wings all who are on the fleet." *Fabrics and Fabrications: The Myth and the Making of William and Mary,* ed. Paul Hoftijzer and C. C. Barfoot, DQR Studies in Literature 6 (Amsterdam: Rodopi, 1990).
6. Edmund Burke, *Reflections on the Revolution in France* (London: Methuen, 1905), 157.
7. Burke, *Letters on a Regicide Peace.* Schama provides an excellent summary of the excremental imagery used against the Dutch. (See Schama, *Riches,* 263–64.)
8. "The Reflection," *Poems on Affairs of State,* ed. W. J. Cameron (New Haven, CT: Yale University Press, 1971), 5:60. "Bardasha" refers to a male homosexual partner.

9. "The Coronation Ballad," *Poems on Affairs of State,* 5:42.

10. *Poems on Affairs of State,* 5:153; "The Shash," 38.

11. John Miller, *The Life and Times of William and Mary* (London: Weidenfeld and Nicolson, 1974) 183, 181–83, 55–56.

12. Henri van der Zee and Barbara van der Zee, *William and Mary* (London: Macmillan, 1973), 415–24. This otherwise sensible and well-documented biography is exemplary, in this respect, of what Foucault called the taking of "sex as the universal secret" *Foucault Live, (Interviews, 1966–1984),* trans. John Johnston, ed. Sylvere Lotringer (New York: Semiotexte, 1989), 144.

13. "A Litany for the Reducing of Ireland: The Second Part," *Poems on Affairs of State,* 5:221. A certain weariness creeps into the editor's comments at this point: "Hans Willem Bentinck, Earl of Portland, is, as usual, accused of homosexual relations with King William." Note too that the author of this poem gives Mary and Anne Stuart the nationalities of their husbands.

14. David Hume, "The Protestant Succession," in *Political Essays,* ed. Knud Haakonssen (Cambridge: Cambridge University Press, 1994), 213–14.

15. Michel Foucault, "Friendship as a Way of Life," in *Foucault Live.*

16. Michel Foucault, "An End to the Monarchy of Sex," in *Foucault Live,* 138.

17. Foucault, "Friendship as a Way of Life," 206.

18. Schama, *Riches,* 95. Hezekiah triumphed against insurmountable odds and an imperial opponent (2 Kings 18:1–8). The choice of Hezekiah is given additional resonance by Proverbs 25:2 and 25:28.

19. Schama, *Riches,* 99.

20. *Poems on Affairs of State,* 5:151.

21. He had been advised by General Monk to go to Breda, rather than returning from Spanish territories. William would not be the first English king to come to the throne from the Low Countries. Ivan Roots, *The Great Rebellion* (London: B. T. Batsford, 1966), 254.

22. Roots, *The Great Rebellion,* 247.

23. Lois Schwoerer provides a systematic and detailed account of William's influence on the Declaration of Rights in in *The Declaration of Rights, 1689* (Baltimore, MD: Johns Hopkins Univ. Press, 1981).

24. Antonio Negri, *The Savage Anomaly,* trans. Michael Hardt (Minneapolis: University of Minnesota Press, 1991), 194.

## CHAPTER 10

1. Friedrich Nietzsche, *On the Genealogy of Morals,* trans. Walter Kaufmann (New York: Vintage, 1969), Second Essay.

2. Saint Just at the trial of Louis Capet, December 27, 1792, quoted in Michael Walzer, *Regicide and Revolution* (Cambridge: Cambridge University Press, 1974), 76.

3. Michel Foucault, *Discipline and Punish,* trans. Alan Sheridan (New York: Vintage Books, 1979), 201.

4. Michel Foucault, *Power/Knowledge,* ed. Colin Gordon (New York: Pantheon, 1972), 152.

5. Some striking examples of these are given in Maurice Agulhon, *Marianne into Battle,* trans. Janet Lloyd (New York: Cambridge University Press, 1981).

6. Christopher Hibbert, *The Days of the French Revolution* (New York: William Morrow, 1980), 92, 174–178.

7. Romilly, *Thoughts on the Probable Influence of the French Revolution on Great Britain,* quoted in Ronald Paulson, *Representations of Revolution* (New Haven: Yale University Press, 1983), 43–47.

8. Edmund Burke, *Reflections on the Revolution in France* (London: Methuen, 1905).

9. Thomas Carlyle, *The French Revolution: A History* (New York: Oxford University Press, 1989), 2:452, 453.

10. "Louis crachant dans le sac." Clery, M. *Journal decequi s'est passé a la tour de Temple* (Paris: Meveuve de France, 1987), 42.
11. "Le bourreaux est assez bien pour lui." Ibid.
12. "Cela ne me regarde point, je suis ici pour conduire à l'echafaud." Ibid.
13. Hibbert, *Days*, 266.
14. Nietzsche, *Genealogy*, Second Essay, 61 and passim. I discuss Nietzsche's account of the sealing of promises and polities in violence in *Reflections on Political Identity* (Baltimore: Johns Hopkins University Press, 1988), chapter 4.
15. See Freud, *Totem and Taboo* (New York: W. W. Norton, 1950), and Anne Norton, *Reflections on Political Identity*, chapter 4.
16. "Nous saurons mettre le gros cochon au regime." *Clery*, 42.
17. Foucault, *Power/Knowledge*, 223.
18. Robespierre, speech before the Convention Nationale, December 28, 1792, in Walzer, *Regicide and Revolution*, 184, my emphasis.
19. De Lally Tollendal, quoted in Burke, *Reflections*, 67 n.2.
20. Burke, *Reflections*, 68.
21. Lynn Hunt discusses the play with this image in *Politics*, 107–110.
22. Carlyle, *The French Revolution*, 2:334.
23. Ibid., 2:205.
24. Ibid., 2:446.
25. Sigmund Freud, *Group Psychology and the Analysis of the Ego*, trans. James Strachey (New York: W. W. Norton, 1959).
26. Ibid., 26.
27. Foucault, *Discipline and Punish*, 217.

## CHAPTER 11

1. Thomas Carlyle, *The French Revolution: A History* (New York: Oxford University Press, 1989), 2: 172, 188, 197.
2. Carlyle, *The French Revolution*, 296. Carlyle adds "of what other malady this History had rather not name," implying that he might have acquired it from the "squalid-Washerwoman, one may call her" with whom he shared a home. In his account of the death of Marat, Carlyle is at pains to link his disease and death to his openness to women.
3. The emphasis on Marat in the letter appears in the painting. Charlotte Corday is not the only petitioner present. The paper Marat has set aside is an assignat prepared for the relief of a widow and her children.
4. Dorothy Johnson, *Jacques-Louis David: Art in Metamorphosis* (Princeton: Princeton University Press, 1993), 14.
5. Ibid.
6. "There are sublime gestures that all of oratorical eloquence will never render." Ibid. Johnson discusses the influence of Diderot on David in chapter 1, "The Eloquent Body," 11–69.
7. Jean-Jacques Rousseau, *On the Origin of Language*, trans. John Moran (Chicago: Univ. of Chicago Press, 1986). Dorothy Johnson discusses David's representations of language in several paintings, attributing his regard for writing to his disillusionment with oratory in the course of the Revolution. See Johnson, *David*, 86–88.
8. David, "Andromache Mourning Hector," 1783, Louvre (Johnson, *David*, plate 11).
9. Thomas Crow, "Revolutionary Activism and the Cult of Male Beauty in the Studio of David," in Bernadette Fort, ed., *Fictions of the French Revolution* (Evanston: Northwestern University Press, 1991), 62–63.
10. Like David's *Marat*, this painting also evokes the East—not by internal referents, but through suggestions that it was painted for a Turkish sultan.
11. Quoted in Dorinda Outram, *The Body and the French Revolution* (New Haven: Yale University Press, 1989), 121.

12. Quoted in Daniel Arasse, *The Guillotine and the Terror,* trans. Christopher Miller (London: Penguin 1989), 39.
13. Ibid.
14. Plato, *Symposium,* in *Lysis Symposium Gorgias,* ed. V. R. M. Lamb (Cambridge: Harvard University Press, 1975).

## CHAPTER 12

1. Gilles Deleuze, *Coldness and Cruelty,* trans. Jean McNeil, published with *Venus in Furs* by Leopold von Sacher-Masoch in *Masochism* (New York: Zone Books, 1989), 16.
2. Marquis de Sade, *The Complete Justine, Philosophy in the Bedroom, and Other Writings,* trans. Richard Seaver and Austryn Wainhouse (New York: Grove Press, 1965), 249.
3. Ibid.
4. Ibid., 265, 226, 363–64.
5. Jules Michelet, *Histoire de France* XIII:25, quoted in Roland Barthes, *Michelet,* trans. Richard Howard (New York: Farrar, Straus and Giroux, 1987), 136–37. Note the curiously symmetrical centrality of the anal in accounts of Louis and William. For William, it is the site of pleasure, for Louis the site of pain; for William the site of love, for Louis the site of war and enmity.
6. Guy Hocqengham, *Homosexual Desire,* trans. Daniella Dangoor (London: Allison and Busby, 1978), 82. Hocqengham here deprecates the social role of the anal "Whereas the phallus is essentially social, the anus is essentially private."
7. Gilles Deleuze and Felix Guattari, *Anti-Oedipus,* quoted in Hocquengham, *Homosexual Desire,* 82.
8. Sade, "Philosophy in the Bedroom," in *The Complete Justine,* 365, 227, 233, 233, 364.
9. Quoted in Stephen Greenblatt, *Learning to Curse* (New York: Routledge, 1990). As Greenblatt observes, Luther's imagery was striking in an age far more scatological than our own. See also Erik Erikson, *Young Man Luther.* (New York: W. W. Norton, 1982).
10. Isaac Kramnick, *Edmund Burke: Portrait of an Ambivalent Conservative* (New York: Basic Books, 1977). For another reading of the oral and anal imagery of the French Revolution, see Ronald Paulson, *Representations of Revolution (1789–1820)* (New Haven: Yale University Press, 1983), 188–202.
11. William Connolly's fine commentary on Sade's relation to Hobbes, Rousseau, and modernity in *Political Theory and Modernity* (Oxford: Basil Blackwell, 1988) foregrounds Sade's refusal to "domesticate desire" (p. 72) and his "demolition of the standard of nature" (p. 79). Connolly explores the distinction between pornography and other forms of writing, and the relation of those regulative irregularities to the modern governance of the body, the self, and the bodies of women.
12. Georges Bataille, quoted in Deleuze, *Coldness and Cruelty,* 17.
13. Deleuze, *Coldness and Cruelty,* 17.
14. Ibid., 18.
15. Ibid., 18–19.
16. Ibid., 20.
17. Ibid.
18. Ibid. I am indebted to Eric Ronshausen for drawing my attention to Deleuze's work on Sacher-Masoch, and for his own commentary on it.
19. *Venus in Furs,* 195–96. Carole Pateman, in *The Sexual Contract* (Stanford CA: Stanford University Press, 1988) suggests that the liberal insistence on taking contracts for consent is often belied not only by the conditions under which the contracts are drawn up but by the provisions of the contracts themselves.

## CHAPTER 13

1. For the British, see C. V. Wedgwood, *A Coffin for King Charles* (New York: Time-Life, 1966), 124.
2. "On ne peut point regner innocemment." David Jordan, *The King's Trial* (Berkeley: University of California Press, 1981), vii, 68.

3. Saint Just at the trial of Louis Capet, December 27, 1792, quoted in *Regicide and Revolution: Speeches at the Trial of Louis XVI,* ed. Michael Walza, trans. Marian Rothstein (New York: Columbia University Press, 1992), 76.

4. Frantz Fanon, *The Wretched of the Earth,* trans. Constance Farrington (New York: Grove Press, 1968), 44–45.

5. Ibid.

6. Sartre's preface to Fanon, *Wretched,* 30.

7. Fanon, *Wretched,* 37.

8. Ibid. This passage prefigures Foucault's suggestion that perhaps we should aim "not to discover who we are, but to refuse who we are." Michel Foucault, "Afterword: The Subject and Power," in Herbert L. Dreyfus and Paul Rabinow, eds., *Michel Foucault: Beyond Structuralism and Hermeneutics* (Chicago: University of Chicago Press, 1982), 216.

9. Fanon, *Wretched,* 86, 36–37.

10. Ibid., 93.

11. Ibid., 94.

12. This view has its most profound and persuasive articulation in Homi Bhabha, *The Location of Culture,* (NY: Routledge, 1994), 40–65.

13. Fanon, *Wretched,* 256.

14. Ibid., 257–58.

15. Ibid., 258.

16. Ibid., 257–58.

17. Ibid., 267.

18. Ibid., 268.

19. Ibid., 262–63.

20. Ibid.

21. See Jacques Lacan, "The Signification of the Phallus," in *Ecrits* (New York: W. W. Norton, 1977), 289.

22. Fanon, *Wretched,* 263.

23. Ibid., 264.

24. Luce Irigaray, *Marine Lover of Friedrich Nietzsche,* trans. Gillian Gill (New York: Columbia University Press, 1991), 102.

25. Fanon, *Wretched,* 253.

26. Genesis 17:5–8. God also gives Abraham land in this passage.

27. Jacques Derrida, *The Gift of Death,* trans. David Wills (Chicago: University of Chicago Press, 1995), 72.

28. Ibid.

29. Ibid., 68–69.

30. Ibid., 73. Yehuda Amichai writes "The real hero of the Binding of Isaac was the ram" "The Real Hero" in *Selected Poetry of Yehuda Amichai,* trans. Chana Bloch and Shephen Mitchell (Berkeley: University of California Press 1996) 156.

31. Ibid., 72.

## CHAPTER 14

1. Carlyle, *The French Revolution: A History* (New York: Oxford University Press, 1989), 1:142, 143.

2. Ibid., 2:259, 1:85–86, 142, 144, 439, 317, 426, 2:387, 390, 398.

3. Ibid., For cannibalism (a recurring theme), see 2:50, 153, 344, 376, 377, 382, 383. For blackness, see 2:53, 64, 84, 98, 115, 329, 377, 386, 389. Tigers, see 2:104, 129. These citations are not exhaustive.

4. Ibid., 1:145.

5. Ibid., 2:55, 387.

6. Ibid., 2:405.

7. These and like characterizations are discussed in Ronald Paulson, *Representations of Revolution (1789–1820)* (New Haven: Yale University Press, 1983), 97–98, and more

extensively in chapter 4, "Blake's Lamb-Tiger," 88–110; in Stewart Crehan, *Blake in Context* (Dublin: Gill and Macmillan, 1984), 127–28, and chapter 5, "Blake's Tyger and the Tygerish Multitude," 123–36. Both are influenced by David Erdman's reading of Blake's tiger; see his *Blake: Prophet Against Empire* (Princeton: Princeton University Press, 1954), 103, 165, 179, 181, 245.

8. Carlyle, *The French Revolution,* 2:56, 198, 211, 396–397, 407, 422, 424, 333. The formula "Mumbo is Mumbo and Robespierre is his Prophet" is, of course, a mockery of the Muslim profession of faith.

9. Ibid., 1:143, 231, 2:198, 199, 210, 211, 383, 405, 404, 403.

10. Ibid., 1:141, 2:407.

11. Ibid., 1:46.

12. Ibid., 2:383, 385, 387. Carlyle contrasts the feline, feminine Robespierre, maker of formulas, with the masculine "Reality" of Danton. "For France there is this Danton only that could still try to govern France. He only, the wild amorophous Titan—and perhaps that other olive-complexioned individual, the Artillery Officer at Toulon." Carlyle had earlier offered a similar assessment of Mirabeau, another Titan. Carlyle marks him as one who might have "become their *king* . . . For a king or leader they, as all bodies of men must have" (1:144, 442–45). Napoleon, Mirabeau, and Danton have the qualities Carlyle ascribed to Cromwell, the qualities of the "canny man" whose masculine regard for reality stands in opposition to the ghostly abstractions and logic-formulas of Robespierre. Carlyle makes the contrast between Cromwell and Robespierre on this score explicit (2:407).

13. Ibid., 2:389.

14. Ibid., 1:145, 147, 443, 447, 448.

15. Ibid., 1:142.

16. Ibid., 1:142, 143, 148; 2:344.

17. Ibid., 1:314, 2:29.

18. Ibid., 2:30.

19. Ibid., 2:376.

20. Ibid., 2:152.

21. Jean Baudrillard, *Simulations,* trans. Paul Foss, Paul Patton, and Philip Beitchman (New York: Semiotexte, 1983), 84, 85. Baudrillard's preoccupation with the relation between counterfeiting and fashion tends to diminish the significance of the relation between counterfeiting and democracy. Burke and Carlyle, who, despite their disparate political positions, display a common distrust of revolution and democracy, identify and employ metaphors of fashion and clothing in their condemnations of revolutionary "excesses."

22. William Blake, "The Four Zoas," in *William Blake,* ed. Michael Mason (Oxford: Oxford University Press, 1994), 454.

23. William Blake, "The Little Black Boy," in *The Poems of William Blake,* ed. W. H. Stevenson, text by David Erdman (London: Longman, 1971), 58.

24. Ibid.

25. William Blake, "America," in *The Poems of William Blake,* ed. W. H. Stevenson, text by David Erdman (London: Longman, 1971), 190.

26. David Erdman, *Blake: Prophet Against Empire,* 213–214. Erdman's work is invaluable for its recognition (and careful delineation) of the connections Blake saw between forms and sites of political oppression, and for his intelligent interpretation of Blake's view of sexual freedom.

27. William Blake, "The Book of Los," in *The Poems of William Blake,* ed. W. H. Stevenson, text by David Erdman (London: Longman, 1971), 280.

28. Richard Price, *A Discourse on the Love of Our Country* (Oxford: Woodstock Books, 1992), 51.

29. William Blake, "Jerusalem" in *Poems,* 176.

30. William Blake, "The French Revolution," in *Poems* 128.

31. Blake, "America," 190, 196.

32. Erdman, *Blake,* 232.

33. *Blake,* "The Four Zoas," in *Poems,* 460.

34. William Blake, "Visions of the Daughters of Albion," in *Poems,* 179, 180, 181.

35. Friedrich Nietzsche, *On the Genealogy of Morals,* trans. Walter Kaufmann (New York: Vintage, 1969), 61, 65; Anne Norton, *Reflections on Political Identity* (Baltimore: Johns Hopkins University Press, 1988), 181–184.

36. William Blake, "The Tiger," in *Poems of William Blake,* 214–15. The treatment of this poem as a commentary on revolution is well established. See Paulson, *Representations,* chapter 4, "Blake's Lamb-Tiger"; Crehan, *Blake in Context,* chapter 5, "Blake's Tyger and the Tygerish Multitude"; and Erdman, *Blake,* passim.

37. Mary Wollstonecraft, "Vindication of the Rights of Man," in *Political Writings,* ed. Janet Todd (London: William Pickering, 1993), 62–63.

38. Alexis de Tocqueville, *Democracy in America,* trans. George Lawrence (New York: Harper Collins, 1988) 2:704.

39. Blake, "The Book of Los," 278.

## CHAPTER 15

1. Carlyle, *The French Revolution: A History* (Oxford: Oxford University Press, 1989), 2:189.

2. Ibid., 2:147, 378, 430. See also 2:54, 259, 282.

3. Ibid., 1:142.

4. Ibid., 2:323, 18–19.

5. Ibid., 1:318, 330, 356.

6. Ibid., 2:147.

7. See also Thomas Carlyle, *Oliver Cromwell* (London: Hutchinson, 1905), 265.

8. Carlyle, *The French Revolution,* 2:378.

9. Ibid., 2:352.

10. Ibid., 2:213.

11. Friedrich Nietzsche, *The Gay Science,* trans. Walter Kaufman (New York: Random House, 1974), 67.

12. Carlyle, *The French Revolution,* 2:335.

13. Edmund Burke, *Letters on a Regicide Peace.*

14. Carlyle, *The French Revolution,* 2:335.

15. Helene Cixous, "The Laugh of the Medusa," in *New French Feminisims,* Elaine Marks and Isabelle de Courtivron, eds., (New York: Schocken Books, 1980), 252.

16. Ibid., 258, 256.

17. Ibid., 255.

18. Ibid., 248, 247.

19. Ibid., 250.

20. Ibid., 245.

21. Ibid., 246.

22. Ibid., 251.

23. Ibid., 249.

24. Jürgen Habermas, "Modernity's Consciousness of Time and Its Need for Self-Reassurance," in *The Philosophical Discourse of Modernity: Twelve Lectures,* trans. Frederick Lawrence (Cambridge, Mass.: MIT Press, 1987), 5.

25. Cixous, *New French Feminisms,* 253.

26. Ibid., 252.

## CHAPTER 16

1. Friedrich Nietzsche, *The Gay Science,* trans. Walter Kaufmann (New York: Vintage Books, 1974), preface to the second edition, 38. He raises this question again in the preface to *Beyond Good and Evil,* trans. Walter Kaufman (New York: Vintage Books, 1966): "Supposing truth is a woman—what then?"

2. C. Kerenyi, *The Gods of the Greeks* (London: Thames and Hudson, 1985), 242.

3. This account is taken principally from Kerenyi. The phrase "uncomely womb" is his. I have also consulted the accounts given in Sarah Kofman, "Baubo: Theological Perversion and Fetishism," trans. Tracy Strong, in Michael Gillespie and Tracy Strong, eds., *Nietzsche's New Seas* (Chicago: University of Chicago Press, 1988), Erich Neumann, *The Great Mother* (Princeton: Princeton University Press, 1963), and Georges Devereux, *Baubo: La vulve mythique* (Paris: Jean-Cyrille Godefroy, 1983).

4. Devereux, *Baubo,* 10. Devereux has a useful discussion of plates and of the various classical sources, 27–36. This work is, however, tendentious and possessed of an unusually crude sexism.

5. Sigmund Freud, *Introductory Lectures on Psychoanalysis,* trans. James Strachey (New York: W. W. Norton, 1977), 317–18.

6. Devereux, *Baubo,* 176.

7. Nietzsche, *Beyond Good and Evil,* Part One, 1. Here the woman appears in the form of the Sphinx.

8. Kerenyi, *Gods,* 244.

9. Ibid., 274.

10. Jean-Jacques Rousseau, *On the Origin of Languages,* trans. John Moran (Chicago: University of Chicago Press, 1986).

## CHAPTER 17

1. Genesis 14:16.
2. Genesis 15:2–6.
3. Genesis 12:1–2.
4. Genesis 13:15.
5. Genesis 16:13–16.
6. Genesis 17:5–8.
7. Genesis 17:10–14.
8. Genesis 18:9–10.
9. Genesis 18:12–15.
10. Luke 1:13, 20, 63–80.
11. Luke 1:20.
12. Luke 1:63–80.
13. Luke 1:41–45.
14. John 1:3–4.
15. John 1:13–14.
16. Jeremiah 1:4–5, 9–10.
17. Ezekiel 3:1–3.

## CHAPTER 18

1. Nietzsche, *The Gay Science,* trans. Walter Kaufmann (New York: Random House, 1974).

2. Freud, *Introductory Lectures on Psychoanalysis,* 318.

3. Foucault, whose writings seem to record the thoroughgoing triumph of the Logos over the body likewise looked to the body for escape and redemption. For Foucault, it was through pleasure, and perhaps through pain, that one escaped authority. Michel Foucault, *Foucault Live,* trans. John Johnston, Sylvere Lotringer, ed. (New York: Semiotexte, 1989), 206.

4. Luce Irigaray, *Marine Lover of Friedrich Nietzsche,* trans. Gillian Gill (New York: Columbia University Press, 1991), 248.

5. Anne Norton, *Reflections on Political Identity* (Baltimore: Johns Hopkins University Press, 1988).

6. Irigaray, *Marine Lover,* 9.

7. Ibid., 19.

8. See Jacques Derrida, *Of Grammatology,* trans. Gayatri Spivak (Baltimore: Johns Hopkins University Press), 165, 150–51.

9. Irigaray, *Marine Lover,* 5.

10. Ibid.

11. Ibid., 4.

12. Ibid., 46.


## CHAPTER 19

1. Jacques Derrida, "Circonfession," in Geoffrey Bennington and Jacques Derrida, *Jacques Derrida,* trans. Geoffrey Bennington (Chicago: University of Chicago Press, 1993), 65–66.

2. Ibid., 68–69.

3. Ibid., 69.

4. Geoffrey Bennington and Jacques Derrida, *Jacques Derrida* (Chicago: University of Chicago Press, 1993), 1.

5. Luce Irigaray, *Marine Lover of Friedrich Nietzsche* (New York: Columbia University Press, 1991), 81.

6. Nietzsche, *The Gay Science,* quoted in Irigaray, *Marine Lover,* 81–82. Nietzsche observes, "The man of letters is essentially an actor."

7. Irigaray, *Marine Lover,* 82.

8. Ibid., 4. See also 78–79, on veiling and the connection to writing; 91–92 on discourse and the woman as "absolute"; 93 on veiling as repression.

9. Ibid., 20.

10. Ibid., 39.

11. Ibid., 83.

12. Derrida, "Circonfession," 65–66.

# Index